A Complete Guide to

Crochet Stitches

A Complete Guide to

Crochet Stitches

A BASIC GUIDE TO CROCHET WORK AND
COMPLETE INSTRUCTIONS FOR OVER 100
STITCH PATTERNS SUITABLE FOR YARNS

MARY M. DAWSON

General Publishing Company Limited, Toronto

General Publishing Company Limited
30 Lesmill Road, Don Mills, Ontario

ISBN 0-7736-1010-3

Photographs: *Robert C. Ragsdale*

Printed in Canada

CONTENTS

SHELLS

LACEY PATTERNS

FANCY PATTERNS

ARAN PATTERNS

MOTIFS

TUNISIAN OR AFGHAN CROCHET

EDGINGS

INTRODUCTION

Until recent years, crochet was almost exclusively worked with crochet cotton for making tablecloths, doilies, bedspreads, and fine edgings for mats and handkerchiefs. Garments, except for fine blouses and baby outfits, were seldom crocheted, and knitting books only called for crochet as edgings around the neck and cuffs of knitted garments. Many experienced knitters never attempted crochet at all and the two crafts were considered as different as the materials they required. This is not the case today. Crocheting with wool and similar yarns has become increasingly popular and fashionable. Patterns are now available for all types of garments from men's sweaters to evening gowns and bikinis. Nor are we restricted to using fine yarns. Many of today's fashions are designed for bulky yarns and double strands of yarn.

Only five basic stitches are used and these are explained and illustrated in the following pages. The purpose of this book is to show the many attractive combinations of these stitches that can be used for crocheting with wool and similar yarns.

The basic terms used in crochet are the same in all English-speaking countries, but the interpretation of the terms is not the same in North America and Britain, and this may cause confusion to anyone who is not aware of it. This book is written according to the North American interpretation (which is accepted in both Canada and the United States). The British equivalents are given on page 11.

The samples shown in this book were made from a medium weight yarn. No tensions are given, or hook sizes suggested, since these can only be determined according to the yarn being used and the type of fabric required. Crochet hooks are usually made of aluminum, plastic, or steel. The steel hooks are very fine and are used mainly for working with crochet cotton. The aluminum and plastic hooks range in size from fine to very coarse and are used for varying weights of yarn. Many different brands of hooks are available in North America, some sized by numbers and some by letters. It is advisable to collect a set of hooks of whichever brand is available in your locality, so that you can adjust your hook size to give you the type of fabric you want.

In crocheting garments it is advisable to have the fabric firm but pliable. A garment made from a fine yarn with too large a hook will not keep its shape well, and the pattern will tend to become lost among the oversized loops of the stitches. A heavy yarn crocheted with too small a hook will produce a fabric that is stiff and heavy and does not show the pattern to the best advantage.

All the samples in this book were made by working back and forth across the rows to give a flat piece of fabric. Circular crochet, where each round is worked in the same direction, is not practical for making garments, except in the case of a seamless skirt. For any garment that has to be divided for armholes or neck openings, it would be necessary to break the circle and work back and forth across a certain portion of the fabric when these openings are reached. This would immediately change the appearance of the pattern since every alternate row would be worked in the opposite direction and, therefore, would show the back of the stitches. However, circular crocheting can be used provided you turn at the end of each round and work the next round in the opposite direction.

As can be seen from the photographs, when working back and forth across the rows in crochet, every alternate row shows the back or wrong side of the stitches. This does not detract from the appearance of the pattern in a great many cases. However, in patterns with long stitches and shells, for example, where the difference between the right side and the wrong side is more apparent, this problem can be eliminated by working a row of smaller stitches, such as single crochet, between each row of shells or long stitches (see page 57).

Note: In the patterns that follow, the multiple of stitches given refers to the multiple required in the **rows of crochet**. This is written in brackets. The extra chain stitches given after the brackets are worked only in the **foundation chain** in order to make the turn into the foundation row. This turning chain, and all subsequent turning chains at the end of each row, **always count as the first stitch in the next row**. The rows following the foundation row frequently begin with: "Miss first st." This means the last stitch of the previous row, and you do not work into it as it is accounted for by the turning chain. For example: If you are working across six stitches your next row will consist of one turning chain and five stitches.

ABBREVIATIONS

ch   = chain
ss   = slip stitch
sc   = single crochet
dc   = double crochet
hdc   = half double crochet
tr   = treble crochet
yoh   = yarn over hook
st, sts = stitch, stitches
inc   = increase
dec   = decrease

TERMINOLOGY

British		North American
chain	=	chain
single crochet or slip stitch	=	slip stitch
double crochet	=	single crochet
half treble	=	half double crochet
treble	=	double crochet
long or double treble	=	treble

HOW TO CROCHET

Beginner's instructions for basic stitches

1. To make first loop: Follow the arrows and lay yarn on Figure A. Put crochet hook in place as shown in Figure A.

Figure B shows yarn and hook of Figure A held in hands.

Pick them up to match picture.

Pull the end-of-yarn and yarn-from-ball in opposite directions as shown in Figure C to tighten loop on hook. This secures first loop on hook. Be sure that it is not too tight or too loose.

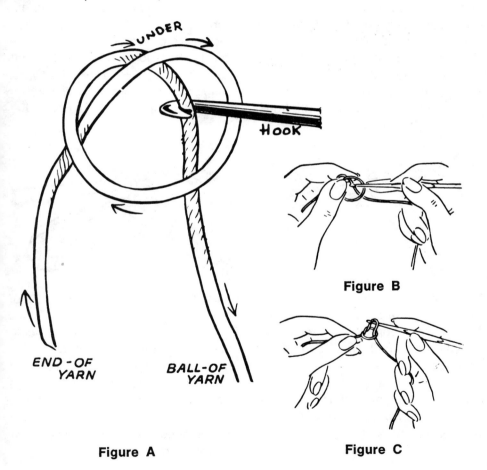

Figure B

Figure C

Figure A

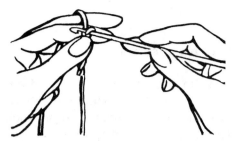

2. How to hold work: Hold **hook** as a pencil is held between first finger and thumb of right hand, but let 2nd finger rest near point.

Hold **work** between first finger and thumb of left hand.

Hold **yarn** by passing it over first and 2nd fingers of left hand, under 3rd and around 4th. Some find it easier to omit the wind around 4th finger when crocheting with yarn.

4. Slip stitch: Make a length of ch. Miss ch next to hook. *Pass hook through next ch. Yoh and draw a loop through both the ch and the loop on hook. This completes 1 ss. Repeat from * to end of ch.

This is the shortest in height of all crochet sts. It is used chiefly for joinings or in fancy patterns where the least noticeable st is desired.

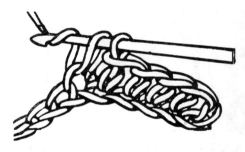

3. Chain: Pass yarn over hook as shown in picture and draw a loop through the loop already on hook. Repeat this until you can do it readily.

This procedure of putting yarn over hook and drawing a loop through the loop or loops already on hook is the basic action in all crochet.

5. Single crochet: Make a length of ch.

First row: Miss ch next to hook. *Pass hook through next ch. Yoh and draw a loop through. Yoh and draw a loop through both loops on hook. This completes 1 sc. Repeat from * to end of ch. Ch 1. Turn work around and you are ready for 2nd row and next picture.

14

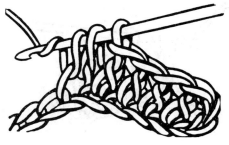

6. Flat surface in sc: 2nd and successive rows: Pass hook under both strands of first sc of previous row. Yoh and draw a loop through. Yoh and draw a loop through both loops on hook. Repeat this in every sc of previous row. At end of row, ch 1. Turn.

8. Half double crochet: Make a length of ch.

First row: Miss 2 ch which will make first st. *Yoh and draw a loop through next ch. Yoh and draw a loop through all 3 loops on hook. This completes 1 hdc. Repeat from * to end of ch. Ch 2. Turn.

2nd and successive rows: Miss first st as the ch 2 at end of previous row counts as first hdc. *Yoh and pass hook under **both** strands of next st. Yoh and draw a loop through all 3 loops on hook. Repeat from * to end of row, working last hdc in top of turning ch of previous row. Ch 2. Turn.

7. Ridged surface in sc: Work in sc as given for flat surface, but instead of passing hook under both strands of an sc pass it under the **back** strand only.

15

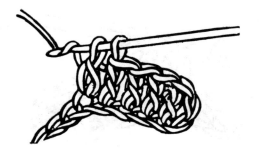 

9. Double crochet: Make a length of ch.

First row: Miss 3 ch which will make first st. *Yoh and draw a loop through next ch. Yoh and draw a loop through first 2 loops on hook. Yoh and draw a loop through remaining 2 loops. This completes 1 dc. Repeat from * to end of ch. Ch 3. Turn.

2nd and successive rows: Miss first st as the ch 3 at end of previous row counts as first dc. *Yoh and pass hook under both strands of next st. Yoh and complete the dc as on first row. Repeat from * to end of row, working last dc in top of turning ch of previous row. Ch 3. Turn.

10. Treble crochet: Make a length of ch.

First row: Miss 4 ch which will make first st. *Yoh twice and draw a loop through next ch. Yoh and draw a loop through first 2 loops on hook. Yoh and draw a loop through next 2 loops. Yoh and draw a loop through remaining 2 loops. This completes 1 tr. Repeat from * to end of ch. Ch 4. Turn.

2nd and successive rows: Miss first st as the ch 4 at end of previous row counts as first tr. *Yoh twice and pass hook under **both** strands of next st. Yoh and complete the tr as on first row. Repeat from * to end of row, working last tr in top of turning ch of previous row. Ch 4. Turn.

Increasing and decreasing

To increase 1 st: Work twice into same st. This may be done at either end of work, or at intervals along row as required. To increase by several sts at end of row, make required number of extra ch sts plus turning chains according to stitch being worked (e.g., 1 extra chain for sc, 2 extra chains for hdc, etc.). Work back across new ch sts, then continue along row as before. See Figures A and B.

Figure A

Figure B

To decrease 1 st: Miss 1 st at beginning or end of row. When working sc, this method may also be used at required intervals along row. When working in larger sts, this method is likely to leave a space that will be noticeable, and the following method is more satisfactory.

17

To decrease in dc: Work 1 dc to 2 loops on hook. 1 dc in next st to 3 loops on hook. Yoh and draw through all 3 loops. (2 sts are now joined at top to form 1 st.) See Figure C.

Figure C

To decrease in tr: Work 1 tr to 2 loops on hook. 1 tr in next st to 3 loops on hook. Yoh and draw through all 3 loops. (2 sts are now joined at top to form 1 st.)

To decrease several sts at end of row: Work to the number of sts to be decreased. Turn, and work back over remaining sts. See Figure D.

Figure D

18

To decrease several sts at beginning of row: Ss over number of sts to be decreased. Make required number of ch sts according to size of st being used, and work over remaining sts. See Figure E.

Figure E

Buttonholes

When buttonholes are required in a crocheted garment they are often readily available without having to be made, because so many crocheted patterns are lacey and open. For example, when making a shell border around the edges of a cardigan, the hole at the base of the shell can be used as a buttonhole.

When using a pattern with tr or dc, the spaces between the sts can also serve as buttonholes.

For solid patterns, it is necessary to make the buttonholes as follows: Work in pattern to buttonhole position. Ch 2. Miss 2 sts. (For larger buttonhole: Ch 3. Miss 3 sts.) Work to end of row. **Next row:** Work in pattern, working over ch sts in same way as other sts in row.

To join motifs

Motifs can be joined by either sewing or crocheting them together. For motifs other than square ones, sewing is the simplest method since they can only be joined at certain points or sides where they meet. See Figure A. The ridge between the motifs is formed by sewing through **back loops only** of the sts along sewn edges.

Figure A

To crochet motifs together place them back to back carefully so that the corresponding sts meet. Work ss along edge, inserting hook through 1 st of each motif. For a flatter seam, the ss may be worked through **front loops only** of edge sts. See Figure B.

Figure B

STITCH PATTERNS

SOLID PATTERNS

1. SINGLE CROCHET (sc)

(Any multiple of sts) plus 1 ch.

Foundation row: 1 sc in 2nd ch from hook. 1 sc in each ch to end of ch. Ch 1. Turn.

2nd row: Miss first st. 1 sc in each st of previous row, ending with 1 sc in turning ch. Ch 1. Turn.

Repeat 2nd row.

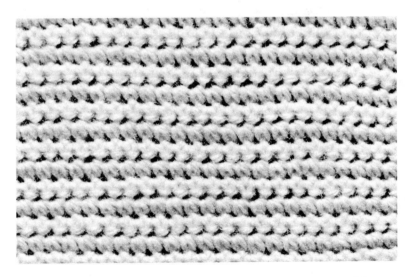

2. HALF DOUBLE CROCHET (hdc)

(Any multiple of sts) plus 1 ch.

Foundation row: 1 hdc in 3rd ch from hook. 1 hdc in each ch to end of ch. Ch 2. Turn.

2nd row: Miss first st. 1 hdc in each st of previous row, ending with 1 hdc in top of turning ch. Ch 2. Turn.

Repeat 2nd row.

3. DOUBLE CROCHET (dc)

(Any multiple of sts) plus 2 ch.

Foundation row: 1 dc in 4th ch from hook. 1 dc in each ch to end of ch. Ch 3. Turn.

2nd row: Miss first st. 1 dc in each st of previous row, ending with 1 dc in top of turning ch. Ch 3. Turn.

Repeat 2nd row.

4. TREBLE (tr)

(Any multiple of sts) plus 3 ch.

Foundation row: 1 tr in 5th ch from hook. 1 tr in each ch to end of ch. Ch 4. Turn.

2nd row: Miss first st. 1 tr in each st of previous row, ending with 1 tr in top of turning ch. Ch 4. Turn. Repeat 2nd row.

5. ALTERNATING ROWS OF dc AND sc

(Any multiple of sts) plus 2 ch.

Foundation row: Work as given for foundation row in pattern No. 3, ending with ch 1. Turn.

2nd and alternate rows: Work as given for 2nd row in pattern No. 1, ending with ch 3. Turn.

3rd and alternate rows: Work as given for 2nd row of pattern No. 3, ending with ch 1. Turn.

6. ALTERNATING ROWS OF tr AND hdc

(Any multiple of sts) plus 3 ch.

Foundation row: Work as given for foundation row of pattern No. 4, ending with ch 2. Turn.

2nd and alternate rows: Work as given for 2nd row of pattern No. 2, ending with ch 4. Turn.

3rd and alternate rows: Work as given for 2nd row of pattern No. 4, ending with ch 2. Turn.

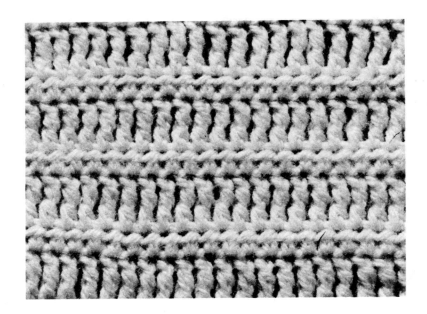

7. ALTERNATING ROWS OF dc AND hdc WITH RIDGES

(Any multiple of sts) plus 2 ch.

Foundation row: Work as given for foundation row of pattern No. 3, ending with ch 2. Turn.

2nd and alternate rows: Work as given for 2nd row of pattern No. 2, ending with ch 3. Turn.

3rd and alternate rows: Working into **back loop only** of each st, work as given for 2nd row of pattern No. 3, ending with ch 2. Turn.

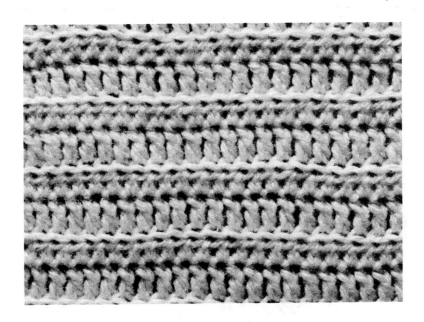

8. BRICK STITCH

(Multiple of 4 sts) plus 1 ch.

Work 2 rows sc as pattern No. 1.

3rd row: Miss first st. *1 sc in each of next 3 sts. Insert hook in foundation ch directly beneath next st and draw up a loop to make next st. Repeat from * to end of row. Ch 1. Turn.

4th and 6th rows: Miss first st. 1 sc in each st to end of row. Ch 1. Turn.

5th row: Miss first st. 1 sc in next st. *Insert hook in st 2 rows below next st and draw up a long loop. 1 sc in each of next 3 sts. Repeat from * ending last repeat with 1 sc in each of last 2 sts. Ch 1. Turn.

Repeat 4th to 6th rows inclusive.

9. MOSS STITCH

(Multiple of 2 sts plus 1) plus 1 ch.

Foundation row: (1 sc. 1 dc) in 2nd ch from hook.
*Miss 1 ch. (1 sc. 1 dc) in next ch. Repeat from *
to end of ch. Ch 1. Turn.

2nd row: Miss first 2 sts. (1 sc. 1 dc) in each dc to
end of row. Ch 1. Turn.

Repeat 2nd row.

10. CROSSED DOUBLES

(Multiple of 2 sts plus 1) plus 1 ch.

Foundation row: 1 dc in 4th ch from hook. 1 dc in 3rd ch from hook. *Miss 1 ch. 1 dc in next ch. 1 dc in missed ch. Repeat from * to end of ch. Ch. 2. Turn.

2nd row: Miss first 2 sts. 1 dc in 3rd st. 1 dc in 2nd st. *Miss 1 st. 1 dc in next st. 1 dc in missed st. Repeat from * to end of row. Ch 2. Turn.
Repeat 2nd row.

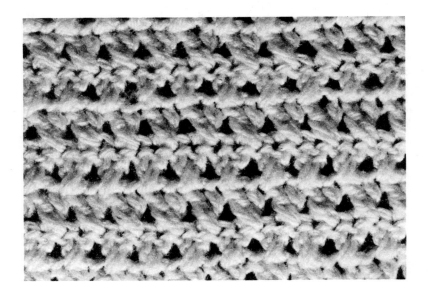

11. CROSSED TREBLES

(Multiple of 2 sts plus 1) plus 2 ch.

Foundation row: 1 tr in 5th ch from hook. 1 tr in 4th ch from hook. *Miss 1 ch. 1 tr in next ch. 1 tr in missed ch. Repeat from * to end of ch. Ch 3. Turn.

2nd row: Miss first 2 sts. 1 tr in 3rd st. 1 tr in 2nd st. *Miss 1 st. 1 tr in next st. 1 tr in missed st. Repeat from * to end of row. Ch 3. Turn.

Repeat 2nd row.

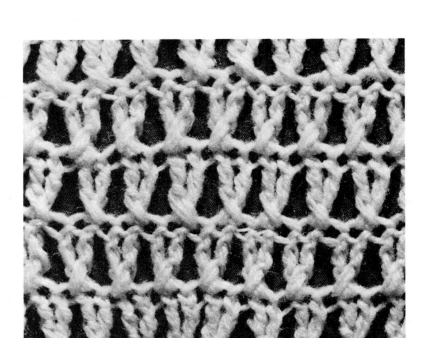

12. POINT STITCH

(Multiple of 2 sts) plus 1 ch.

Foundation row: Miss 2 ch. *Draw a loop through each of next 2 ch. Yoh and draw through first 2 loops. Yoh and draw through last 2 loops. Ch 1. Repeat from * to end of ch. Turn.

2nd row: Miss first st. 1 sc in each st to end of row. 1 sc in turning ch. Ch 2. Turn.

3rd row: Miss first st. *Draw a loop through each of next 2 sts and join as given in foundation row. Ch 1. Repeat from * to end of row. Turn.

Repeat 2nd and 3rd rows.

13. FANCY DOUBLES

(Multiple of 2 sts plus 1) plus 2 ch.

Foundation row: 1 dc in 3rd ch from hook to 2 loops on hook. *Miss 1 ch. 1 dc in next ch to 3 loops on hook. Yoh and draw through remaining 3 loops. Ch 1. 1 dc in same st to 2 loops on hook. Repeat from * to last 2 ch. Miss 1 ch. 1 dc in last ch to 3 loops on hook and draw through remaining 3 loops. Ch 3. Turn.

2nd row: 1 dc in first st to 2 loops. Work as given for foundation row from * having last dc in top of turning ch. Ch 3. Turn.

Repeat 2nd row.

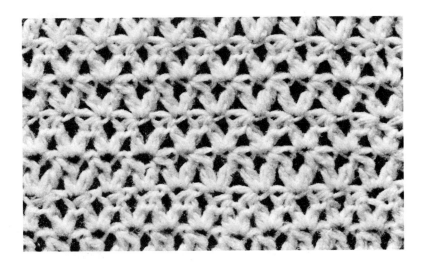

14. ALTERNATING SHELLS

(Multiple of 6 sts plus 1) plus 2 ch.

Foundation row: 4 dc in 3rd ch from hook. *Miss 2 ch. 1 sc in next ch. Miss 2 ch. 5 dc in next ch. Repeat from * to last 3 ch. Miss 2 ch. 3 dc in last ch. Turn.

2nd row: 1 sc in first st. Miss 2 dc. *5 dc in next sc. 1 sc in 3rd dc of next shell. Repeat from * ending with 3 dc in top of last st.

Repeat 2nd row.

SPACES AND SQUARES

15. Sc WITH ch 1 SPACES

(Multiple of 2 sts plus 1) plus 2 ch.

Foundation row: 1 sc in 3rd ch from hook.   *Ch 1. Miss 1 ch.   1 sc in next ch.   Repeat from * to end of ch.   Ch 3.   Turn.

2nd row: Miss first 2 sts.   *1 sc in next sc.   Ch 1. Repeat from * ending with 1 sc in 2nd st of turning ch. Ch 3.   Turn.

Repeat 2nd row.

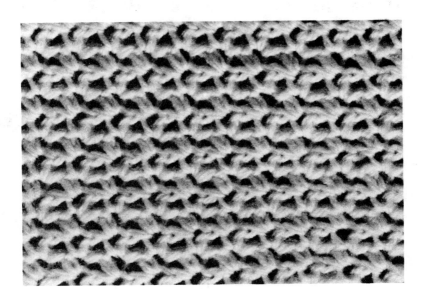

16. Hdc WITH ch 1 SPACES

(Multiple of 2 sts plus 1) plus 3 ch.

Foundation row: 1 hdc in 4th ch from hook. *Ch 1. Miss 1 ch. 1 hdc in next ch. Repeat from * to end of ch. Ch 3. Turn.

2nd row: Miss first 2 sts. *1 hdc in next hdc. Ch 1. Repeat from * ending with 1 hdc in 2nd st of turning ch. Ch 3. Turn.

Repeat 2nd row.

17. Dc WITH ch 1 SPACES

(Multiple of 2 sts plus 1) plus 2 ch.

Foundation row: 1 dc in 5th ch from hook. *Ch 1. Miss 1 ch. 1 dc in next ch. Repeat from * to end of ch. Ch 4. Turn.

2nd row: Miss first 2 sts. *1 dc in next dc. Ch 1. Repeat from * ending with 1 dc in 3rd st of turning ch. Ch 4. Turn.

Repeat 2nd row.

18. Dc WITH ch 2 SPACES

(Multiple of 3 sts plus 1) plus 2 ch.

Foundation row: 1 dc in 6th ch from hook. *Ch 2. Miss 2 ch. 1 dc in next ch. Repeat from * to end of ch. Ch 5. Turn.

2nd row: Miss first 3 sts. *1 dc in next dc. Ch 2. Repeat from * ending with 1 dc in 3rd st of turning ch. Ch 5. Turn.

Repeat 2nd row.

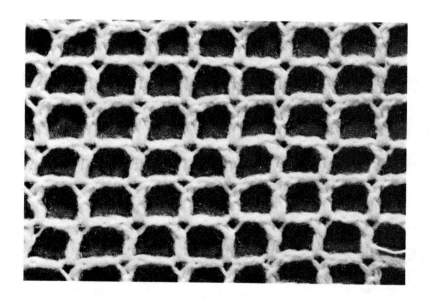

19. Tr WITH ch 1 SPACES

(Multiple of 2 sts plus 1) plus 1 ch.

Foundation row: 1 tr in 6th ch from hook. *Ch 1. Miss 1 ch. 1 tr in next ch. Repeat from * to end of ch. Ch 5. Turn.

2nd row: Miss first 2 sts. *1 tr in next tr. Ch 1. Repeat from * ending with 1 tr in 4th st of turning ch. Ch 5. Turn.

Repeat 2nd row.

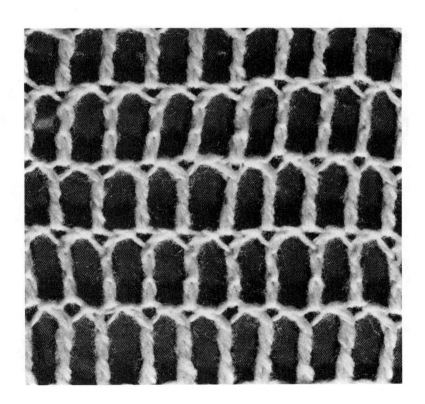

20. Tr WITH ch 2 SPACES

(Multiple of 3 sts plus 1) plus 3 ch.

Foundation row: 1 tr in 7th ch from hook. *Ch 2. Miss 2 ch. 1 tr in next ch. Repeat from * to end of ch. Ch 6. Turn.

2nd row: Miss first 3 sts. *1 tr in next tr. Ch 2. Repeat from * ending with 1 dc in 3rd st of turning ch. Ch 6. Turn.

Repeat 2nd row.

21. Dc WITH ch 2 BLOCKS

(Multiple of 4 sts plus 2) plus 2 ch.

Foundation row: 1 dc in 4th ch from hook. *Ch 2. Miss 2 ch. 1 dc in each of next 2 ch. Repeat from * to end of ch. Ch 4. Turn.

2nd row: Miss first 2 dc. 1 dc in each ch st. *Ch 2. Miss 2 dc. 1 dc in each ch st. Repeat from * to last 2 dc. Ch 2. Miss 1 dc. 1 dc in top of turning ch. Ch 3. Turn.

3rd row: Miss first st. 1 dc in next ch st. *Ch 2. Miss 2 dc. 1 dc in each ch st. Repeat from * to last 2 dc. Ch 2. Miss 2 dc. 1 dc in top of turning ch, then 1 dc in next st of turning ch. Ch 4. Turn.

Repeat 2nd and 3rd rows.

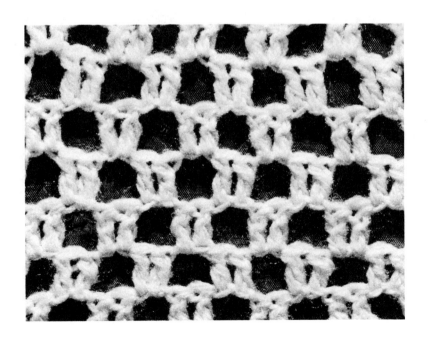

22. Tr WITH ch 3 BLOCKS

(Multiple of 6 sts plus 3) plus 3 ch.

Foundation row: 1 tr in 5th ch from hook. 1 tr in next ch. *Ch 3. Miss 3 ch. 1 tr in each of next 3 ch. Repeat from * to end of ch. Ch 7. Turn.

2nd row: *Miss first 3 sts. 1 tr in each ch st. Repeat from * to last 3 sts. Ch 3. Miss 2 sts. 1 tr in top of turning ch. Ch 4. Turn.

3rd row: Miss first st. 1 tr in each of next 2 ch. *Ch 3. Miss 3 sts. 1 tr in each ch st. Repeat from * ending with 1 tr in each of first 3 ch of turning ch. Ch 7. Turn.

Repeat 2nd and 3rd rows.

23. SQUARES WITH SPACES (A)

(Multiple of 8 sts plus 3) plus 2 ch.

Foundation row: 1 dc in 4th ch from hook. 1 dc in each ch to end of ch. Ch 4. Turn.

2nd row: Miss first 2 sts. 1 dc in next st. *Ch 1. Miss 1 st. 1 dc in next st. Repeat from * ending with 1 dc in top of turning ch. Ch 4. Turn.

3rd row: Miss first dc and ch 1. *1 dc in each of next 7 sts. Ch 1. Miss 1 st. Repeat from * to turning ch. Miss first st of turning ch. 1 dc in 2nd st of turning ch. Ch 4. Turn.

4th and 5th rows: As 3rd row.

Repeat 2nd to 5th rows inclusive.

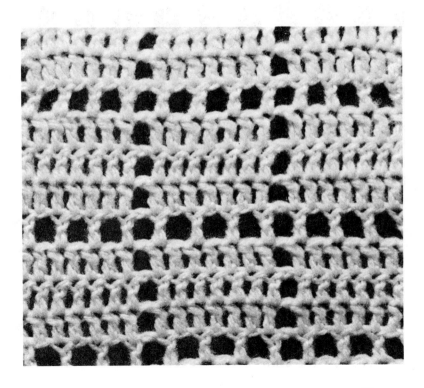

24. SQUARES WITH SPACES (B)

(Multiple of 4 sts plus 3) plus 2 ch.

Foundation row: 1 dc in 4th ch from hook. 1 dc in each ch to end of ch. Ch 4. Turn.

2nd row: Miss first 2 sts. 1 dc in next st. *Ch 1. Miss 1 st. 1 dc in next st. Repeat from * ending with 1 dc in top of turning ch. Ch 4. Turn.

3rd row: Miss first dc and ch 1. *1 dc in each of next 3 sts. Ch 1. Miss 1 st. Repeat from * to turning ch. Miss first st of turning ch. 1 dc in 2nd st of turning ch. Ch 4. Turn.

4th row: As 3rd row.

Repeat 2nd to 4th rows inclusive.

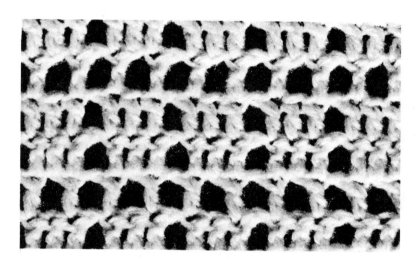

25. WEB PATTERN

(Multiple of 11 sts plus 1) plus 2 ch.

Foundation row: 1 dc in 4th ch from hook. *(Miss 1 ch. Ch 2. 1 dc in next ch)5 times. 1 dc in next ch. Repeat from * to end of ch. Ch 3. Turn.

2nd row (right side): Miss first st. *1 dc in next dc. Ch 4. 1 hdc in each of next 4 dc. Ch 4. 1 dc in next dc. Repeat from * ending with 1 dc in top of turning ch. Ch 3. Turn.

3rd row: Miss first st. *1 dc in next dc. Ch 4. 1 sc in each of next 4 hdc. Ch 4. 1 dc in next dc. Repeat from * ending with 1 dc in top of turning ch. Ch 3. Turn.

4th row: Miss first st. *1 dc in next dc. Ch 4. 1 sc in each of next 4 sc. Ch 4. 1 dc in next dc. Repeat from * ending with 1 dc in top of turning ch. Ch 3. Turn.

5th row: As 4th row.

6th row: Miss first st. *1 dc in next dc. (Ch 2. 1 hdc in next sc)4 times. Ch 2. 1 dc in next dc. Repeat from * ending with 1 dc in top of turning ch. Ch 3. Turn.

7th row: Miss first st. *1 dc in next dc. (Ch 2. 1 dc in next hdc)4 times. Ch 2. 1 dc in next dc. Repeat from * ending with 1 dc in top of turning ch. Ch 3. Turn.

Repeat 2nd to 7th rows inclusive.

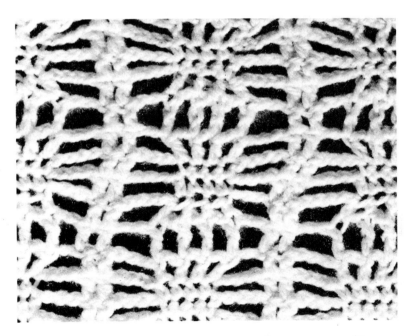

SHELLS

Note: All shell patterns give instructions for a half shell at each end of the row so that if two pieces of the finished fabric are joined for side seams, etc., the two halves make a complete shell.

26. SIMPLE dc SHELLS

(Multiple of 5 sts plus 1) plus 2 ch.

Foundation row: 1 dc in 3rd ch from hook. Miss 4 ch. *5 dc for shell in next ch. Miss 4 ch. Repeat from * to last ch. 3 dc in last ch. Ch 3. Turn.

2nd row: 2 dc in first st. *Shell in 3rd dc of each shell, ending with 2 dc in top of turning ch. Ch 3. Turn.

3rd row: 1 dc in first st. *Shell in 3rd dc of each shell, ending with 3 dc in top of turning ch. Ch 3. Turn.

Repeat 2nd and 3rd rows.

27. SPLIT dc SHELLS

(Multiple of 5 sts plus 1) plus 2 ch.

Foundation row: 1 dc in 3rd ch from hook. Miss 4 ch. *(2 dc. Ch 1. 2 dc) for shell in next ch. Miss 4 ch. Repeat from * to last ch. 2 dc in last ch. Ch 3. Turn.

2nd row: 1 dc in first st. Shell in ch 1 space of each shell, ending with 2 dc in top of turning ch. Ch 3. Turn.

Repeat 2nd row.

28. SIMPLE tr SHELLS

(Multiple of 5 sts plus 1) plus 3 ch.

Foundation row: 1 tr in 4th ch from hook. Miss 4 ch. *5 tr for shell in next ch. Miss 4 ch. Repeat from * to last ch. 3 tr in last ch. Ch 4. Turn.

2nd row: 2 tr in first st. Shell in 3rd tr of each shell, ending with 2 tr in top of turning ch. Ch 4. Turn.

3rd row: 1 tr in first st. Shell in 3rd tr of each shell, ending with 3 tr in top of turning ch. Ch 4. Turn. Repeat 2nd and 3rd rows.

29. SPLIT tr SHELLS

(Multiple of 5 sts plus 1) plus 3 ch.

Foundation row: 2 tr in 4th ch from hook. Miss 4 ch. *(3 tr. Ch 1. 3 tr) for shell in next ch. Miss 4 ch. Repeat from * to last ch. 3 tr in last ch. Ch 4. Turn.

2nd row: 2 tr in first st. Shell in ch 1 space of each shell, ending with 3 tr in top of turning ch. Ch 4. Turn.

Repeat 2nd row.

30. OPEN dc SHELLS

(Multiple of 5 sts plus 1) plus 3 ch.

Foundation row: 1 dc in 4th ch from hook. *Miss 4 ch. (1 dc. Ch 1)3 times, 1 dc for shell in next ch. Repeat from * ending with (1 dc. Ch 1. 1 dc) in last ch. Ch 4. Turn.

2nd row: 1 dc in first ch 1 space. Shell in 2nd ch 1 space of each shell, ending with (1 dc. Ch 1. 1 dc) in last ch 1 space. Ch 4. Turn.

Repeat 2nd row.

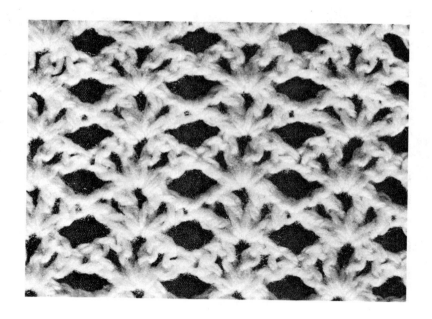

31. OPEN tr SHELLS

(Multiple of 6 sts plus 1) plus 4 ch.

Foundation row: 1 tr in 5th ch from hook. *Miss 5 ch. (1 tr. Ch 1)3 times, 1 tr for shell in next ch. Repeat from * ending with (1 tr. Ch 1. 1 tr) in last ch. Ch 5. Turn.

2nd row: 1 tr in first ch 1 space. Shell in 2nd ch 1 space of each shell, ending with (1 tr. Ch 1. 1 tr) in last ch 1 space. Ch 5. Turn.

Repeat 2nd row.

32. SHELLS INCREASING

(Multiple of 5 sts plus 1) plus 2 ch.

Foundation row: 1 dc in 4th ch from hook. Miss 4 ch. *(2 dc. Ch 1. 2 dc) for shell in next ch. Miss 4 ch. Repeat from * to last ch. 2 dc in last ch. Ch 3. Turn.

2nd row: 2 dc in first st. (3 dc. Ch 1. 3 dc) in each ch 1 space, ending with 3 dc in top of turning ch. Ch 5. Turn.

3rd row: 2 tr in first st. (3 tr. Ch 1. 3 tr) in each ch 1 space, ending with 3 tr in top of turning ch. Ch 5. Turn.

4th row: 3 tr in first st. (4 tr. Ch 2. 4 tr) in each ch 1 space, ending with 4 tr in top of turning ch. Ch 5. Turn.

5th row: 4 tr in first st. (5 tr. Ch 2. 5 tr) in each ch 2 space, ending with 5 tr in top of turning ch. Ch 6. Turn.

6th row: (1 tr. Ch 1)3 times, 1 tr all in first st. (1 tr. Ch 1)5 times, ch 1, (1 tr. Ch 1)4 times, 1 tr all in each ch 2 space, ending with (1 tr. Ch 1)4 times, 1 tr all in top of turning ch. Ch 6. Turn.

7th row: (1 tr. Ch 1)4 times, 1 tr all in first st. (1 tr. Ch 1)6 times, ch 1, (1 tr. Ch 1)5 times, 1 tr all in each ch 2 space, ending with (1 tr. Ch 1)5 times, 1 tr all in top of turning ch.

33. Dc SHELLS AND BARS

(Multiple of 6 sts plus 1) plus 2 ch.

Foundation row: 1 dc in 3rd ch from hook. *Miss 2 ch. 1 dc in next ch. Miss 2 ch. 5 dc for shell in next ch. Repeat from * to last 6 ch. Miss 2 ch. 1 dc in next ch. Miss 2 ch. 3 dc in last ch. Ch 3. Turn.

2nd row: 2 dc in first st. Miss 2 dc. *1 dc in next dc. Shell in centre dc of next shell. Repeat from * ending with 2 dc in top of turning ch. Ch 3. Turn.

3rd row: 1 dc in first st. Miss 1 dc. 1 dc in next dc. Shell in centre st of next shell. Repeat from * ending with 1 dc in last dc. 3 dc in top of turning ch. Ch 3. Turn. Repeat 2nd and 3rd rows.

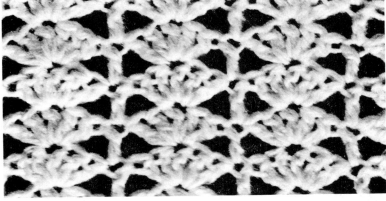

34. Tr SHELLS AND BARS

(Multiple of 6 sts plus 1) plus 3 ch.

Foundation row: 1 tr in 5th ch from hook. *Miss 2 ch. 1 tr in next ch. Miss 2 ch. 5 tr for shell in next ch. Repeat from * to last 6 ch. Miss 2 ch. 1 tr in next ch. Miss 2 ch. 3 tr in last ch. Ch 4. Turn.

2nd row: 2 tr in first st. Miss 2 tr. *1 tr in next tr. Shell in centre st of next shell. Repeat from * ending with 1 tr in last tr. 2 tr in top of turning ch. Ch 4. Turn.

3rd row: 1 tr in first st. Miss 1 tr. *1 tr in next tr. Shell in centre st of next shell. Repeat from * ending with 1 tr in last tr. 3 tr in top of turning ch. Ch 4. Turn.

Repeat 2nd and 3rd rows.

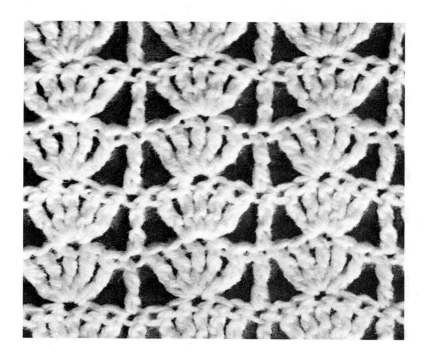

Note: Up to this point, all shell patterns have been worked with shells in **every** row. This means that every alternate row shows the back or wrong side of the shells, since they are worked from the opposite direction. For patterns showing the right side of **all** shells, it is necessary to work back over each shell row with a smaller stitch in order that every shell row is worked in the same direction. Following are examples of shell patterns worked in this manner.

35. Dc SHELLS WITH sc ROW

(Multiple of 5 sts plus 1) plus 1 ch.
Foundation row: 1 sc in 2nd ch from hook. 1 sc in each ch to end of ch. Ch 3. Turn.
2nd row: 1 dc in first st. Miss 4 sts. *5 dc for shell in next st. Miss 4 sts. Repeat from * to last st. 3 dc in last st. Ch 1. Turn.
3rd row: Miss first st. 1 sc in each st of previous row, ending with 2 sc in top of turning ch. Ch 3. Turn.
Repeat 2nd and 3rd rows.

36. Tr SHELLS WITH sc ROW

(Multiple of 5 sts plus 1) plus 1 ch.

Foundation row: 1 sc in 2nd ch from hook.   1 sc in each ch to end of ch.   Ch 4.   Turn.

2nd row: 1 tr in first st.   Miss 4 sts.   *5 tr for shell in next st.   Miss 4 sts.   Repeat from * ending with 3 tr in turning ch.   Ch 1.   Turn.

3rd row: Miss first st.   1 sc in each st of previous row, ending with 2 sc in top of turning ch.   Ch 4. Turn.

Repeat 2nd and 3rd rows.

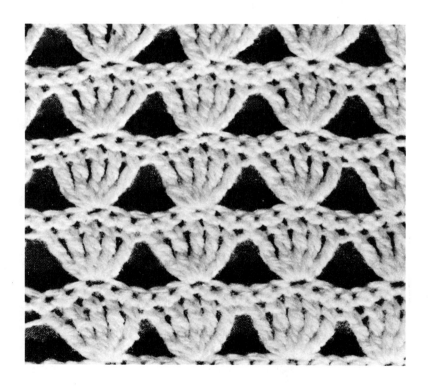

37. OPEN tr SHELLS WITH hdc ROW

(Multiple of 6 sts plus 1) plus 2 ch.

Foundation row: 1 hdc in 3rd ch from hook. 1 hdc in each ch to end of ch. Ch 5. Turn.

2nd row: 1 tr in first st. Miss 5 sts. *(1 tr. Ch 1)4 times, 1 tr for shell in next st. Miss 4 sts. Repeat from * ending with (1 tr. Ch 1)twice, 1 tr in turning ch. Ch 2. Turn.

3rd row: Miss first st. 1 hdc in each st of previous row, ending with 1 hdc in each of 2 top sts of turning ch. Ch 5. Turn.

4th row: 1 tr in first st. Miss 6 sts. *Shell in next st. Miss 8 sts. Repeat from * ending with (1 tr. Ch 1) twice, 1 tr in turning ch. Ch 2. Turn.

Repeat 3rd and 4th rows.

38. Tr SHELLS WITH OPEN hdc ROW

(Multiple of 8 sts plus 1) plus 3 ch.

Foundation row: 1 hdc in 4th ch from hook. *Ch 1. Miss 1 ch. 1 hdc in next ch. Repeat from * to end of ch. Ch 4. Turn.

2nd row: 3 tr in first ch 1 space. Ch 1. Miss 3 ch 1 spaces. *7 tr for shell in next ch 1 space. Ch 1. Miss 3 ch 1 spaces. Repeat from * ending with 4 tr in last space. Ch 3. Turn.

3rd row: Miss first st. *1 hdc in next st. Ch 1. Miss 1 st. Repeat from * ending with 1 hdc in top of turning ch. Ch 4. Turn.

Repeat 2nd and 3rd rows.

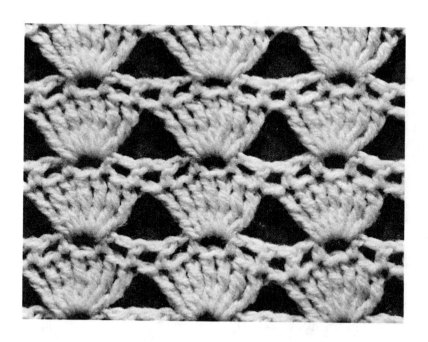

39. LACEY SHELLS

(Multiple of 8 sts plus 2) plus 1 ch.

Foundation row: 1 sc in 2nd ch from hook.   *Ch 1. 1 sc in each of next 4 ch.   Ch 2.   1 sc in each of next 4 ch.   Repeat from * to last 2 ch.   1 sc in each of last 2 ch.   Ch 3.   Turn.

2nd row: *(1 dc.   Ch 2.   1 dc) in ch 1 space.   (2 dc. Ch 1.   2 dc) in ch 2 space.   Repeat from * ending with (1 dc.   Ch 2.   1 dc) in last ch 1 space.   1 dc in turning ch.   Ch 3.   Turn.

3rd row: *(2 dc.   Ch 1.   2 dc) in ch 2 space.   (1 dc. Ch 2.   1 dc) in ch 1 space.   Repeat from * ending with (2 dc.   Ch 1.   2 dc) in last ch 2 space.   1 dc in top of turning ch.   Ch 3.   Turn.

Repeat 2nd and 3rd rows.

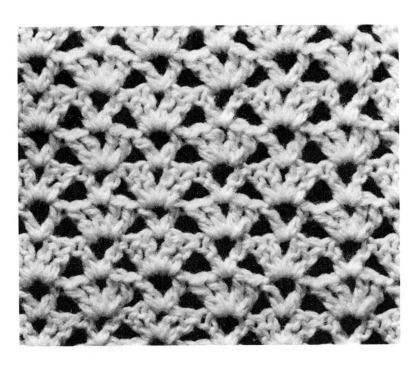

40. ARCH SHELLS

(Multiple of 6 sts plus 1) plus 1 ch.

Foundation row: 1 sc in 2nd ch from hook. 1 sc in next ch. *Ch 3. Miss 3 ch. 1 sc in each of next 3 ch. Repeat from * to last 5 ch. Miss 3 ch. 1 sc in each of last 2 ch. Ch 1. Turn.

2nd row: 1 sc in first st. *5 dc in ch 3 space. Miss 1 sc. 1 sc in next sc. Repeat from * to end of row. Ch 3. Turn.

3rd row: *1 sc in each of 3 centre sts of 5 dc group. Ch 3. Repeat from * ending with ch 2. 1 sc in turning ch. Ch 3. Turn.

4th row: 2 dc in ch 2 space. *1 sc in centre st of 3 sc of previous row. 5 dc in ch 3 space. Repeat from * ending with 3 dc in last ch space. Ch 1. Turn.

5th row: 1 sc in each of first 2 sts. *Ch 3. 1 sc in each of 3 centre sts of 5 dc group. Repeat from * ending with 1 sc in last dc. 1 sc in turning ch. Ch 1. Turn.

Repeat 2nd to 5th rows inclusive.

41. BOXED SHELLS

(Multiple of 6 sts plus 1) plus 4 ch.

Foundation row: 2 tr in 5th ch from hook.   *Miss 2 ch. 1 sc in next ch. Miss 2 ch. 5 tr in next ch for shell. Repeat from * to last 6 ch. Miss 2 ch. 1 sc in next ch. Miss 2 ch. 3 tr in last ch. Ch 4. Turn.

2nd row: Miss 3 tr. *1 tr in next sc. Ch 2. 1 sc in 3rd tr of shell. Ch 2. Repeat from * to last 6 sts. 1 tr in next sc. Ch 2. Miss 2 tr. 1 sc in top of turning ch. Ch 4. Turn.

3rd row: 2 tr in first sc. *1 sc in next tr. Shell in next sc. Repeat from * to last tr. 1 sc in last tr. 3 tr in bottom of turning ch. Ch 4. Turn.

Repeat 2nd and 3rd rows.

42. ALTERNATING dc SHELLS

(Multiple of 6 sts plus 1) plus 3 ch.

Foundation row: 2 dc in 4th ch from hook. *Miss 2 ch. 1 sc in next ch. Miss 2 ch. 5 dc in next ch for shell. Repeat from * to last 6 ch. Miss 2 ch. 1 sc in next ch. Miss 2 ch. 3 dc in last ch. Ch 3. Turn.

2nd row: Miss 3 dc. *1 sc in next sc. Ch 2. 1 sc in 3rd dc of shell. Ch 2. Repeat from * to last 6 sts. 1 sc in next sc. Ch 2. Miss 2 dc. 1 sc in top of turning ch. Turn.

3rd row: 1 sc in first st. *Shell in next sc. 1 sc in next sc. Repeat from * ending with 1 sc in bottom of turning ch. Ch 3. Turn.

4th row: 1 sc in 3rd dc of first shell. *Ch 2. 1 sc in next sc. Ch 2. 1 sc in 3rd dc of next shell. Repeat from * ending with 1 sc in last st. Ch 3. Turn.

5th row: 2 dc in first sc. *1 sc in next sc. Shell in next sc. Repeat from * ending with 3 dc in bottom of turning ch. Ch 3. Turn.

Repeat 2nd to 5th rows inclusive.

43. ALTERNATING tr SHELLS

(Multiple of 6 sts plus 1) plus 4 ch.

Foundation row: 2 tr in 5th ch from hook. *Miss 2 ch. 1 sc in next ch. Miss 2 ch. 5 tr in next ch for shell. Repeat from * to last 6 ch. Miss 2 ch. 1 sc in next ch. Miss 2 ch. 3 tr in last ch. Ch 4. Turn.

2nd row: Miss 3 tr. *1 dc in next sc. Ch 2. 1 sc in 3rd tr of shell. Ch 2. Repeat from * to last 6 sts. 1 dc in next sc. Ch 2. Miss 2 tr. 1 sc in top of turning ch. Turn.

3rd row: 1 sc in first st. *Shell in next dc. 1 sc in next sc. Repeat from * ending with 1 sc in bottom of turning ch. Ch 4. Turn.

4th row: 1 sc in 3rd tr of first shell. *Ch 2. 1 dc in next sc. Ch 2. 1 sc in 3rd tr of next shell. Repeat from * ending with Ch 2. 1 sc in last st. Ch 4. Turn.

5th row: 2 tr in first sc. *1 sc in next sc. Shell in next sc. Repeat from * ending with 3 tr in bottom of turning ch. Ch 4. Turn.

Repeat 2nd to 5th rows inclusive.

44. Ch 2 LACE

(Multiple of 3 sts plus 1) plus 3 ch.

Foundation row: 1 sc in 4th ch from hook. *Ch 2. Miss 2 ch. 1 sc in next ch. Repeat from * to end of ch. Ch 2. Turn.

2nd row: 1 sc in first ch space. *Ch 2. 1 sc in next ch space. Repeat from * ending with 1 sc in last ch space. Ch 2. Turn.

Repeat 2nd row.

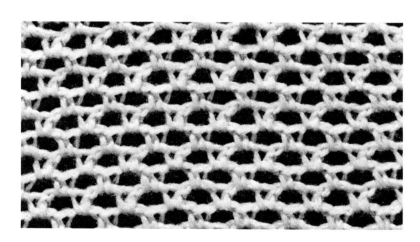

45. Ch 3 LACE

(Multiple of 4 sts plus 1) plus 4 ch.

Foundation row: 1 sc in 5th ch from hook. *Ch 3. Miss 3 ch. 1 sc in next ch. Repeat from * to end of ch. Ch 3. Turn.

2nd row: 1 sc in first ch space. *Ch 3. 1 sc in next ch space. Repeat from * ending with 1 sc in last ch space. Ch 3. Turn.

Repeat 2nd row.

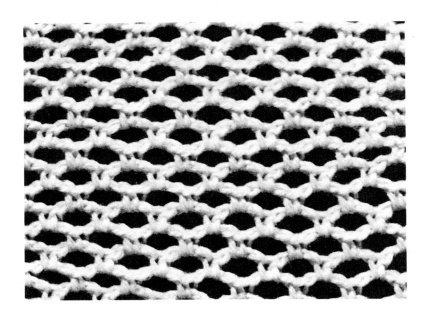

46. Ch 4 LACE

(Multiple of 5 sts plus 1) plus 5 ch.

Foundation row: 1 sc in 6th ch from hook. *Ch 4. Miss 4 ch. 1 sc in next ch. Repeat from * to end of ch. Ch 4. Turn.

2nd row: 1 sc in first ch space. *Ch 4. 1 sc in next ch space. Repeat from * ending with 1 sc in last ch space. Ch 4. Turn.

Repeat 2nd row.

47. Ch 5 LACE

(Multiple of 6 sts plus 1) plus 6 ch.

Foundation row: 1 sc in 7th ch from hook. *Ch 5. Miss 5 ch. 1 sc in next ch. Repeat from * to end of ch. Ch 5. Turn.

2nd row: 1 sc in first ch space. *Ch 5. 1 sc in next ch space. Repeat from * ending with 1 sc in last ch space. Ch 5. Turn.

Repeat 2nd row.

48. LACE WITH SPACED SHELLS

(Multiple of 6 sts plus 1) plus 6 ch.

Foundation row: 1 sc in 7th ch from hook. *Ch 5. Miss 5 ch. 1 sc in next ch. Repeat from * to end of ch. Ch 5. Turn.

2nd row: 1 sc in first ch space. *Ch 5. 1 sc in next ch space. Repeat from * ending with 1 sc in last ch space. Ch 5. Turn.

3rd row: 1 sc in first space. *9 dc for shell in next space. 1 sc in next space. Ch 5. 1 sc in next space. Repeat from * to end of row, being careful to avoid having shell in last space. Ch 5. Turn.

4th row: Work as 2nd row, working over shells as follows: Ch 5. 1 sc in 3rd dc of shell. Ch 5. Miss 2 dc. 1 sc in next dc. Ch 5. 1 sc in next space. Work to end of row. Ch 5. Turn.

5th row: As 2nd row.

6th row: As 3rd row, working shells in spaces between shells of 3rd row.

7th row: As 4th row.

Repeat 2nd to 7th rows inclusive.

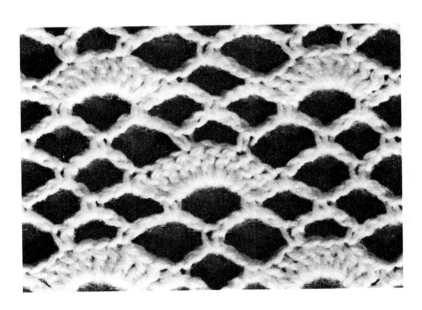

49. LACE WITH ALTERNATING SHELLS

(Multiple of 8 sts plus 2) plus 1 ch.

Foundation row: 1 sc in 2nd ch from hook. 1 sc in next ch. *Ch 2. Miss 2 ch. (1 dc. Ch 3. 1 dc) in next ch. Ch 2. Miss 2 ch. 1 sc in each of next 3 ch. Repeat from * ending with 1 sc in each of last 2 ch. Ch 1. Turn.

2nd row: 1 sc in first sc. *Ch 2. 7 dc in ch 3 space. Ch 2. 1 sc in 2nd sc of 3 sc group. Repeat from * ending with ch 2. 1 sc in last sc. Ch 1. Turn.

3rd row: 1 sc in first sc. Ch 2. *1 sc in each of next 7 dc. Ch 5. Repeat from * ending with ch 2. 1 sc in last sc. Ch 5. Turn.

4th row: 1 dc in first sc. *Ch 2. 1 sc in each of 3rd, 4th and 5th sc of 7 sc group. Ch 2. (1 dc. Ch 3. 1 dc) in 3rd ch of ch 5 space. Repeat from * ending with (1 dc. Ch 3. 1 dc) in last sc. Ch 3. Turn.

5th row: 3 dc in first ch 3 space. *Ch 2. 1 sc in 2nd sc of 3 sc group. Ch 2. 7 dc in ch 3 space. Repeat from * ending with 4 dc in turning ch loop. Ch 1. Turn.

6th row: 1 sc in each of first 4 dc. *Ch 5. 1 sc in each of next 7 dc. Repeat from * ending with ch 5. 1 sc in each of last 3 sc. 1 sc in top of turning ch. Ch 1. Turn.

7th row: 1 sc in each of first 2 sc. *Ch 2. (1 dc. Ch 3. 1 dc) in 3rd ch of ch 5 loop. Ch 2. 1 sc in each of 3rd, 4th and 5th sc of 7 sc group. Repeat from * ending with ch 2. 1 sc in each of last 2 sc. Ch 1. Turn.

Repeat 2nd to 7th rows inclusive.

50. FANCY LACE

(Multiple of 4 sts plus 1) plus 7 ch.

Foundation row: 1 sc in 8th ch from hook. *Ch 3. Miss 3 ch. 1 dc in next ch. Repeat from * to end of ch. Ch 4. Turn.

2nd row: *1 sc in 2nd st of ch 3 of previous row. Ch 2. 1 dc in dc. Ch 2. Repeat from * ending with ch 2. 1 sc in 3rd st of turning ch. Ch 5. Turn.

3rd row: 1 dc in first dc. *Ch 3. 1 dc in next dc. Repeat from * ending with 1 dc in 2nd st of turning ch. Ch 4. Turn.

Repeat 2nd and 3rd rows.

51. LACE WITH PICOTS

(Multiple of 7 sts plus 1) plus 2 ch.

Foundation row: 1 dc in 3rd ch from hook. *Ch 2. Miss 2 ch. 1 sc in next ch. (Ch 3. Ss in first of these 3 ch) for picot. 1 sc in same ch as last sc. Ch 2. Miss 2 ch. 1 dc in each of next 2 ch. Repeat from * to end of ch. Turn.

2nd row: 1 sc between first 2 dc. *Ch 6. 1 sc in ch space after picot. Ch 1. 1 sc in ch space before next picot. Repeat from * ending with ch 1. 1 sc in last st. Turn.

3rd row: 1 sc in first st. *(3 dc. Ch 2. 3 dc) for shell in next ch 6 space. 1 sc in ch between next 2 sc. Repeat from * ending with 1 sc in last st. Turn.

4th row: 1 sc in first st. *Ch 3. (1 sc. Picot. 1 sc) in centre of shell. Repeat from * ending with 2 dc in last st. Turn.

Repeat 2nd to 4th rows inclusive.

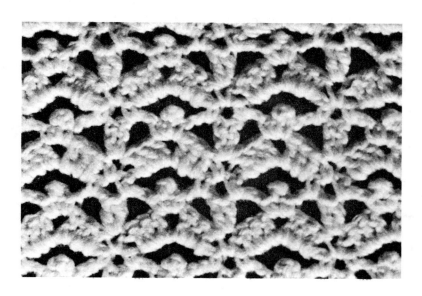

72

52. LATTICES

(Multiple of 3 sts plus 1) plus 4 ch.

Foundation row: (1 tr. Ch 1. 1 tr) for lattice in 5th ch from hook. *Miss 2 ch. Lattice in next ch. Repeat from * to last 3 ch. Miss 2 ch. 1 tr in last ch. Ch 4. Turn.

2nd row: Lattice in each ch 1 space to end of row. 1 tr in top of turning ch. Ch 4. Turn.

Repeat 2nd row.

53. LATTICES WITH sc ROW

(Multiple of 3 sts plus 1) plus 4 ch.

Foundation row: (1 tr. Ch 1. 1 tr) for lattice in 5th ch from hook. *Miss 2 ch. Lattice in next ch. Repeat from * to last 3 ch. Miss 2 ch. 1 tr in last ch. Ch 1. Turn.

2nd row: 1 sc in first st. 1 sc in each st of previous row, ending with 1 sc in top of turning ch. Ch 4. Turn.

3rd row: Miss first 2 sts. *Lattice in next st. Miss 2 sts. Repeat from * ending with 1 tr in top of turning ch. Ch 1. Turn.

Repeat 2nd and 3rd rows.

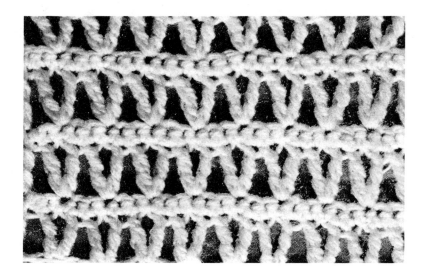

54. ZIG-ZAGS

(Multiple of 4 sts plus 1) plus 1 ch.

Foundation row: 1 sc in 2nd ch from hook. 1 sc in each ch to end of ch. Ch 7. Turn.

2nd row: Miss first 3 sts. 1 sc in next st. *Ch 7. Miss 3 sts. 1 sc in next st. Repeat from * to last 3 sts. Ch 3. 1 tr in turning ch. Ch 1. Turn.

3rd row: 1 sc in first st. Ch 3. 1 sc in 4th st of first ch 7. *Ch 3. 1 sc in 4th st of next ch 7. Repeat from * to last ch 7. Ch 3. 1 sc in 4th st and 1 sc in 5th st of last ch. Ch 1. Turn.

4th row: 1 sc in 2nd sc. *3 sc in ch 3 space. 1 sc in next sc. Repeat from * ending with 1 sc in last sc. 1 sc in top of turning ch. Ch 7. Turn.

Repeat 2nd to 4th rows inclusive.

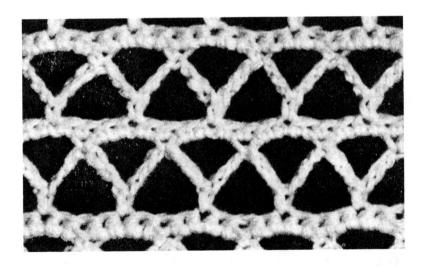

55. DIAMOND LATTICES

(Multiple of 3 sts plus 1) plus 1 ch.

Foundation row: 1 sc in 2nd ch from hook.   1 sc in each ch to end of ch.   Ch 5.   Turn.

2nd row: 1 tr in first st to 2 loops on hook.   Miss 2 sts.   1 tr in next st to 3 loops on hook.   Yoh and draw through remaining 3 loops.   Ch 2.   *1 tr in same st as last tr to 2 loops on hook.   Miss 2 sts.   1 tr in next st to 3 loops on hook.   Yoh and draw through remaining 3 loops.   Ch 2.   Repeat from * ending with 1 tr in last st (same st as last tr).   Ch 3.   Turn.

3rd row: Miss first 3 sts.   1 tr in next st.   Ch 2. Work as given in 2nd row from * having last tr in 3rd st of turning ch.   Ch 5.   Turn.

Repeat 2nd and 3rd rows.

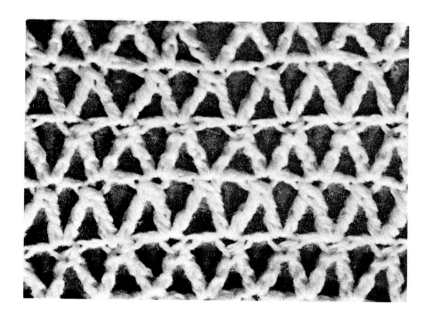

56. CLUSTERS

(Multiple of 2 sts plus 1) plus 1 ch.

Foundation row: 1 sc in 2nd ch from hook. 1 sc in each ch to end of ch. Ch 2. Turn.

2nd row: Miss first st. (Yoh and draw up a loop)4 times in next st. (9 loops on hook). Yoh and draw through all 9 loops for cluster. *Ch 1. Miss 1 st. Cluster in next st. Repeat from * to last st. 1 dc in last st. Ch 2. Turn.

3rd row: Miss first st. Cluster in top of first cluster. *Ch 1. Cluster in next cluster. Repeat from * to end of row. 1 dc in top of turning ch. Ch 2. Turn. Repeat 3rd row.

57. BOBBLES

(Multiple of 2 sts plus 1) plus 1 ch.

Foundation row: 1 sc in 2nd ch from hook.   1 sc in each ch to end of ch.   Ch 2.   Turn.

2nd row: Miss first st.   1 dc in next st to 2 loops on hook.   (This forms 'post'.)   (Yoh and draw up a loop around this post)3 times.   Yoh and draw through all 8 loops to form bobble.   *Ch 1.   Miss 1 st.   Bobble in next st.   Repeat from * to last st.   1 dc in last st. Ch 1.   Turn.

3rd row: Miss first st.   1 sc in each bobble and each ch 1, ending with 1 sc in top of turning ch.   Ch 2. Turn.

4th row: Miss first st.   Bobble in next st.   *Ch 1. Miss 1 st.   Bobble in next st.   Repeat from * to last st. 1 dc in last st.   Ch 1.   Turn.

Repeat 3rd and 4th rows.

58. THREE-COLOUR PATTERN

(Multiple of 4 sts plus 1) plus 1 ch.

Foundation row: With dark colour (D) 1 sc in 2nd ch from hook.   1 sc in each ch to end of ch.   Turn.

2nd row: Ch 3.   1 dc in first st.   *Miss 3 sts.   3 dc in next st.   Repeat from * to last 4 sts.   Miss 3 sts. 2 dc in last st.   Turn.

Join medium colour (M).

3rd row: Ch 2. *3 dc in centre of 3 sts missed in previous row. Repeat from * ending with 1 hdc in centre of ch 3. Turn.

4th row: Ch 3. 1 dc in space between hdc and next group of dc. Inserting hook in centre of dc group 2 rows below, work 3 dc between each group of dc ending with 2 dc in space between last group and ch. Turn.

Join light colour (L).

5th row: Ch 2. 3 dc in each centre dc of group 2 rows below, ending with 1 hdc in centre of ch 3. Turn.

6th row: As 4th row.

7th row: With (D) as 5th row.

8th row: With (D) as 4th row.

9th row: With (M) as 5th row.

Keeping colour sequence, repeat 4th to 9th rows inclusive.

59. RIPPLE PATTERN

(Multiple of 14 sts plus 13) plus 1 ch.

Foundation row: 1 dc in 4th ch from hook. 1 dc in each of next 3 ch. *3 dc in next ch. 1 dc in each of next 5 ch. Miss 1 ch. 1 dc in next ch. Miss 1 ch. 1 dc in each of next 5 ch. Repeat from * to last 6 ch. 3 dc in next ch. 1 dc in each of last 5 ch. Turn.

2nd row: Ch 1. Miss first 2 sts. 1 sc in each of next 4 sts. *3 sc in next st. 1 sc in each of next 5 sts. Miss 1 st. 1 sc in next st. Miss 1 st. 1 sc in each of next 5 sts. Repeat from * to last 7 sts. 3 sc in next st. 1 sc in each of next 4 sts. Miss 1 st. 1 sc in top of turning ch. Turn.

3rd row: Ch 3. Miss first 2 sts. 1 dc in each of next 4 sts. *3 dc in next st. 1 dc in each of next 5 sts. Miss 1 st. 1 dc in next st. Miss 1 st. 1 dc in each of next 5 sts. Repeat from * to last 7 sts. 3 dc in next st. 1 dc in each of next 4 sts. Miss 1 st. 1 dc in top of turning ch. Turn.

Repeat 2nd and 3rd rows.

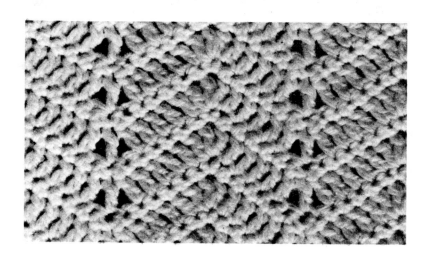

60. RIPPLES IN THREE COLOURS

Main colour (B). Contrasting colours (A) and (C).
With (A) work foundation row and 2nd row as given for ripple pattern.

3rd and 4th rows: With (B) work as 2nd row of ripple pattern.

5th row: With (C) work as 3rd row of ripple pattern.

6th row: With (C) work as 2nd row.

7th and 8th rows: With (B) work as 2nd row.

9th row: With (A) as 3rd row of ripple pattern.

Repeat 2nd to 9th rows inclusive.

61. LOOP STITCH

(Any multiple of sts) plus 1 ch.

Foundation row: 1 sc in 2nd ch from hook. 1 sc in each ch to end of ch. Ch 1. Turn.

2nd row (wrong side): Miss first st. *Insert hook in next st and holding yarn around middle finger of left hand to make loop of desired length, draw yarn through st. Yoh and draw through 2 loops. Slip long loop off finger. Repeat from * to end of row, being careful to keep loops of uniform size. Ch 1. Turn.

3rd row: Miss first st. 1 sc in each st to end of row. Ch 1. Turn.

Repeat 2nd and 3rd rows.

62. RINGS

*Wind yarn around top of left thumb 3 times. Using these 3 strands as a ring, work sufficient sc into ring to cover **one half**. Slip ring off thumb. **Do not break yarn**, but repeat from * for desired number of rings. Work right around last ring, then around uncovered half of each ring back to 1st ring. Ss in first sc. Fasten off.

63. COVERED RINGS

Plastic rings are recommended. Draw a loop through centre of first ring and, working around ring, work sufficient sc to cover **one half** of ring. **Do not break yarn**, but work into next ring. Continue working around one half of desired number of rings to last ring. Work right around last ring, then around uncovered half of each ring back to first ring. Ss in first sc. Fasten off.

64. SHELL LADDERS

(Multiple of 18 sts plus 1) plus 3 ch.

Foundation row: 1 dc in 4th ch from hook.   *Ch 3. Miss 7 ch.   5 dc in next ch.   Ch 2.   1 dc in each of next 5 ch.   Ch 2.   Miss 3 ch.   1 dc in each of next 2 ch.   Repeat from * to end of ch.   Ch 2.   Turn.

2nd row: Miss first st.   1 dc in next st.   *Ch 3.   Miss 2 ch and 5 dc.   5 dc in ch 2 space.   Ch 2.   1 dc in each of next 5 dc.   Ch 2.   Miss 3 ch.   1 dc in each of next 2 sts.   Repeat from * ending last repeat with 1 dc in last st.   1 dc in top of turning ch.   Ch 2.   Turn.

Repeat 2nd row.

65. SHELL CLUSTERS

(Multiple of 12 sts plus 1) plus 4 ch.

Foundation row: 1 dc in 5th ch from hook. *Miss 5 ch. (Ch 2. 1 dc)4 times in next ch. Ch 2. Miss 5 ch. (1 dc. Ch 1. 1 dc) in next ch. Repeat from * to end of ch. Ch 4. Turn.

2nd row (right side): 1 dc in ch 1 space. *Miss one ch 2 space. (1 hdc. 2 dc. 1 hdc) for shell in each of next 3 ch 2 spaces. Miss next ch 2 space. (1 dc. Ch 1. 1 dc) in ch 1 space. Repeat from * to end of row working last (1 dc. Ch 1. 1 dc) in top of turning ch space. Ch 4. Turn.

3rd row: 1 dc in ch 1 space. *(Ch 2. 1 dc)4 times in first dc of 2nd shell. Ch 2. (1 dc. Ch 1. 1 dc) in ch 1 space. Repeat from * to end of row working last (1 dc. Ch 1. 1 dc) in turning ch space. Ch 4. Turn.

Repeat 2nd and 3rd rows.

66. SHELL PANELS

Ch 6.   Join with ss to form ring.

Foundation row: Ch 4.   8 tr in ring.   Ch 4.   Turn.

2nd row: Miss first st.   (1 dc in next st.   Ch 1)8 times.   Turn.

3rd row: 1 sc in first dc.   (Ch 3.   1 sc in next dc)8 times, working last sc in top of turning ch.   Ch 1. Turn.

(First shell made.)

4th row: 10 tr in 3rd ch 3 space.   Miss one ch 3 space.   1 sc in next ch 3 space.   Ch 3.   Turn.

5th row: Miss first tr.   (1 dc in next tr.   Ch 1)9 times. Turn.

6th row: 1 sc in first dc.   (Ch 3.   1 sc in next dc)8 times.   Ch 3.   1 sc in turning ch space.   1 sc in next ch 3 space of previous shell.   Ch 1.   Turn.   (2nd shell made.)

7th row: 10 tr in 2nd ch 3 space of previous shell. Miss one ch 3 space.   1 sc in next ch 3 space of previous shell.   Ch 3.   Turn.

8th row: Miss 1 tr.   (1 dc in next tr.   Ch 1)9 times. 1 sc in next ch 3 space of shell below.   Ch 1.   Turn.

9th row: 1 sc in first dc.   (Ch 3.   1 sc in next dc)8 times.   Ch 3.   1 sc in turning ch space.   1 sc in next ch 3 space of previous shell.   Ch 1.   Turn.   (3rd shell made.)

Repeat 7th to 9th rows inclusive.

Work desired number of panels to desired length and sew together.   With wrong side of work facing, work 1 round sc, working 3 sc in each ch 3 loop and 1 sc between each shell around entire edge.   Fasten off.

67. CLUSTER GROUPS

(Multiple of 10 sts) plus 2 ch.

To make cluster: (Yoh. Draw up a loop one-half inch long in next st. Yoh and draw through first 2 loops on hook)3 times in same st. Yoh and draw through all 4 loops on hook.

Foundation row: 1 hdc in 3rd ch from hook. 1 hdc in each of next 2 ch. *Ch 3. Miss 3 ch. 1 hdc in each of next 7 ch. Repeat from * to last 7 ch. Ch 3. Miss 3 ch. 1 hdc in each of last 4 ch. Ch 2. Turn.

2nd row: 1 hdc in space between first and 2nd hdc. 1 hdc in space between 2nd and 3rd hdc. *Ch 2. (Cluster. Ch 2)twice in ch 3 space. 1 hdc in each of centre 4 spaces between hdc. Repeat from * to last ch 3 space. Ch 2. (Cluster. Ch 2)twice in ch 3 space. 1 hdc in space between last 2 hdc. 1 hdc in turning ch space. Ch 3. Turn.

3rd row: *Ch 2. Cluster in top of cluster. Ch 2. Cluster in ch 2 space. Ch 2. Cluster in top of cluster. Ch 2. 1 dc in space between 2nd and 3rd hdc. Repeat from * ending with 1 dc in turning ch space. Ch 5. Turn.

4th row: *(1 hdc in top of cluster. 2 hdc in ch 2 space)twice. 1 hdc in top of cluster. Ch 3. Repeat from * ending last repeat with ch 2. 1 dc in 3rd st of turning ch. Ch 4. Turn.

5th row: Cluster in ch 2 space. *Ch 2. 1 hdc in each of centre 4 spaces between hdc. (Ch 2. Cluster)twice in ch 3 space. Repeat from * to last pattern. Ch 2. 1 hdc in each of centre 4 spaces between hdc. Ch 2. Cluster in turning ch space. Ch 1. 1 dc in 3rd st of turning ch. Ch 2. Turn.

6th row: 1 dc in ch 1 space. Ch 2. Cluster in top of cluster. *Ch 2. 1 dc in space between 2nd and 3rd hdc. Ch 2. Cluster in top of cluster. Ch 2. Cluster in ch 2 space. Ch 2. Cluster in top of cluster. Repeat from * to last pattern. Ch 2. 1 dc in space between 2nd and 3rd hdc. Ch 2. Cluster in top of cluster. Ch 2. (Yoh and draw up a loop in turning ch space. Yoh and draw through 1st 2 loops on hook) twice. Yoh and draw through all 3 loops on hook. Ch 2. Turn.

7th row: *2 hdc in ch 2 space. 1 hdc in top of cluster. Ch 3. 1 hdc in top of cluster. 2 hdc in ch 2 space. 1 hdc in top of cluster. Repeat from * ending with 1 hdc in last dc. Ch 2. Turn.

Repeat 2nd to 7th rows inclusive.

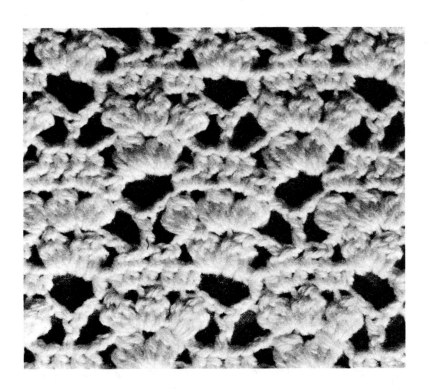

68. CLUSTER FANS

(Multiple of 8 sts plus 1) plus 1 ch.

Foundation row: 1 sc in 2nd ch from hook. *Ch 3. Miss 3 ch. (1 dc. Ch 3. 1 dc) in next ch. Ch 3. Miss 3 ch. 1 sc in next ch. Repeat from * to end of ch. Ch 1. Turn.

2nd row (right side): 1 sc in first sc. *3 sc in ch loop. 1 sc in next dc. 5 sc in next ch loop. 1 sc in next dc. 3 sc in next ch loop. 1 sc in next sc. Repeat from * to end of row. Ch 3. Turn.

3rd row: Miss 5 sc. *(Yoh. Insert hook in next st and draw up a loop about one-half inch long)3 times. Yoh and draw through first 6 loops. Yoh and draw through remaining 2 loops to make cluster. (Ch 3. Cluster in next sc)4 times. Miss 4 sc. 1 tr in next sc. Miss 4 sc. Repeat from * ending with 1 tr in last sc. Ch 1. Turn.

4th row: 1 sc in first tr. *Ch 4. Miss next ch loop. 1 sc in next ch loop. Ch 3. 1 sc in following ch loop. Miss next ch loop. Ch 4. 1 sc in next tr. Repeat from * ending with 1 sc in top of turning ch. Ch 1. Turn.

5th row: 1 sc in first sc. *Ch 3. Miss ch 4 loop. (1 dc. Ch 3. 1 dc) in next ch 3 loop. Ch 3. Miss next ch 4 loop. 1 sc in next sc. Repeat from * to end of row. Ch 1. Turn.

Repeat 2nd to 5th rows inclusive.

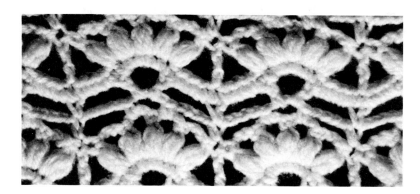

69. CLUSTER STRIPES

(Multiple of 6 sts plus 3) plus 1 ch.

Foundation row: 1 sc in 2nd ch from hook. 1 sc in each ch to end of ch. Ch 3. Turn.

2nd row (right side): Miss first st. 1 dc in each st to end of row. Ch 1. Turn.

3rd row: 1 sc in first st. *1 sc in next st. Ch 3. Miss 2 sts. (Yoh and draw up a loop)4 times in next st. (9 loops on hook.) Yoh and draw through all 9 loops. Ch 1 for cluster. Ch 3. Miss 2 sts. Repeat from * to last 2 sts. 1 sc in next st. 1 sc in top of turning ch. Ch 5. Turn.

4th row: 3 sc in top of first cluster. *Ch 3. 3 sc in top of next cluster. Repeat from * ending with ch 2. 1 dc in last st. Ch 1. Turn.

5th row: 1 sc in each st, ending with 3 sc in each of first 3 sts of turning ch. Ch 3. Turn.

Repeat 2nd to 5th rows inclusive.

70. CLUSTER RIB

(Multiple of 8 sts plus 1) plus 1 ch.

Foundation row: 1 sc in 2nd ch from hook. *Ch 2. Miss 3 ch. (1 dc. Ch 3. 1 dc) in next ch. Ch 2. Miss 3 ch. 1 sc in next ch. Repeat from * to end of ch. Ch 6. Turn.

2nd row: 1 sc in ch 3 space. *Ch 3. (Yoh. Insert hook and draw up a loop about one-half inch long)3 times in next sc. Yoh and draw through all 7 loops. Ch 1 for cluster. Ch 3. 1 sc in ch 3 space. Repeat from * ending with 1 dc in last st. Ch 1. Turn.

3rd row: 1 sc in dc. *Ch 2. (1 dc. Ch 3. 1 dc) in sc. Ch 2. 1 sc in cluster. Repeat from * ending with 1 sc in 3rd st of ch 6. Ch 6. Turn.

Repeat 2nd and 3rd rows.

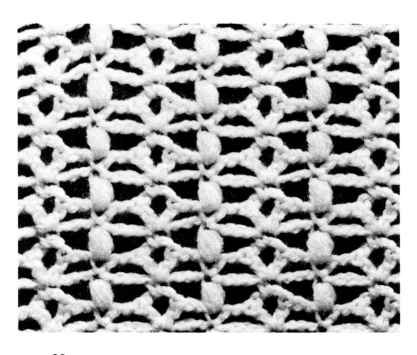

71. MOTIF PATTERN

(Multiple of 14 sts plus 3) plus 1 ch.

Foundation row: 1 sc in 2nd ch from hook. 1 sc in each ch to end of ch. Ch 2. Turn.

2nd row: 1 dc in first 3 sts. *Ch 3. Miss 3 sts. 1 sc in each of next 5 sts. Ch 3. Miss 3 sts. 1 dc in each of next 3 sts. Repeat from * to end of row. Ch 4. Turn.

3rd row: *3 dc in ch 3 space. Ch 3. Miss 1 sc. 1 sc in each of next 3 sc. Ch 3. Miss 1 sc. 3 dc in next ch 3 space. Repeat from * ending with ch 3. 1 dc in top of turning ch of previous row. Ch 3. Turn.

4th row: 1 dc in first ch 3 space. *Ch 3. 3 dc in next ch 3 space. Ch 3. Miss 1 sc. 1 dc in next sc. Ch 3. Miss 1 sc. 3 dc in next ch 3 space. Ch 3. 1 dc **between** the two 3 dc groups. Repeat from * ending with ch 3. 1 dc in last ch 3 space. Ch 1. Turn.

5th row: 1 sc in first dc. 1 sc in first ch 3 space. *Ch 3. 3 dc in each of next 2 ch 3 spaces. Ch 3. 1 sc in next ch 3 space. 1 sc in next dc. 1 sc in next ch 3 space. Repeat from * ending with 1 sc in last ch 3 space. 1 sc in top of turning ch. Ch 1. Turn.

6th row: 1 sc in each of first 2 sc. 1 sc in first ch 3 space. *Ch 3. 3 dc **between** the two 3 dc groups. Ch 3. 1 sc in next ch 3 space. 1 sc in each of next 3 sc. 1 sc in next ch 3 space. Repeat from * ending with 1 sc in last ch 3 space. 1 sc in each of last 2 sc. Ch 1. Turn.

7th row: 1 sc in each of first 2 sc. Miss 1 sc. *Ch 3. 3 dc in each of next 2 ch 3 spaces. Ch 3. Miss 1 sc. 1 sc in each of next 3 sc. Miss 1 sc. Repeat from * ending with 1 sc in each of last 2 sc. Ch 2. Turn.

8th row: 1 dc in first sc. Ch 3. Miss 1 sc. *3 dc in next ch 3 space. Ch 3. 1 dc **between** the two 3 dc groups. Ch 3. 3 dc in next ch 3 space. Ch 3. Miss

1 sc. 1 dc in next sc. Ch 3. Miss 1 sc. Repeat from * ending with ch 3. 1 dc in last sc. Ch 3. Turn.

9th row: *3 dc in ch 3 space. Ch 3. 1 sc in next ch 3 space. 1 sc in next dc. 1 sc in next ch 3 space. Ch 3. 3 dc in next ch 3 space. Repeat from * ending with 3 dc in last ch 3 space. Ch 2. Turn.

10th row: 1 dc in first 3 dc. *Ch 3. 1 sc in next ch 3 space. 1 sc in each of next 3 sc. 1 sc in next ch 3 space. Ch 3. 3 dc **between** the two 3 dc groups. Repeat from * ending with 1 dc in each of last 3 dc. Ch 4. Turn.

Repeat 3rd to 10th rows inclusive.

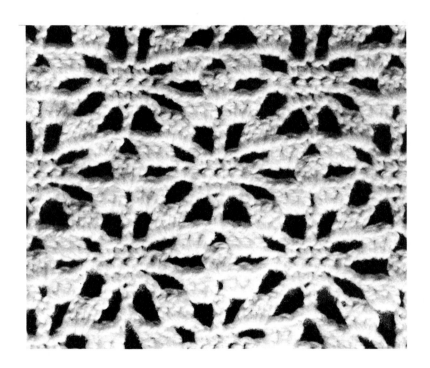

ARAN PATTERNS

72. LATTICE STITCH

(Multiple of 6 sts) plus 1 ch.

Foundation row: 1 sc in 2nd ch from hook. 1 sc in each ch to end of ch. Ch 1. Turn.

2nd row: Miss first st. 1 sc in each st of previous row. Ch 1. Turn.

3rd and 4th rows: As 2nd row.

5th row: Miss first st. 1 sc in next st. (Yoh and draw up a loop one-half inch long around first st on 2nd row. Work this loop as a dc.) (This will be termed long dc.) *Miss next 4 sts on 2nd row. Long dc in next st. Miss next 2 sts on 4th row. 1 sc in each of next 4 sts. Long dc in st on 2nd row adjacent to last long dc. Repeat from * to last 4 sts. Long dc in last st. Miss next 2 sts on 4th row. 1 sc in each of last 2 sts. Ch 1. Turn.

6th, 7th, and 8th rows: As 2nd row omitting ch 1 at end of 8th row.

9th row: Long dc in 4th st on 6th row. Miss first st on 8th row. 1 sc in each of next 4 sts. Long dc in st on 6th row adjacent to last long dc. *Miss next 4 sts on 6th row. Long dc in next st. Miss next 2 sts on 8th row. 1 sc in each of next 4 sts. Long dc in st on 6th row adjacent to last long dc. Repeat from * to last st. 1 sc in last st. Ch 1. Turn.

Repeat 2nd to 9th rows inclusive.

73. CHEVRON STITCH

(Multiple of 6 sts) plus 1 ch.

Work as given for Lattice Stitch, repeating 2nd to 5th rows inclusive.

74. Tr ZIG-ZAGS

(Multiple of 5 sts) plus 1 ch.

Foundation row: 1 sc in 2nd ch from hook. 1 sc in each ch to end of ch. Ch 3. Turn.

2nd row: Miss first st. 1 dc in each st to end of row. Ch 1. Turn.

3rd row: Miss first st. 1 sc in each st to end of row. Ch 3. Turn.

4th row: As 2nd row.

5th row: Yoh twice and draw up a loop one-half inch long around 5th dc of 2nd row. Work this loop as a tr. (This will be termed long tr.) Miss first st on 4th row. *1 sc in each of next 4 sts. Miss 4 sts on 2nd row. Long tr in next st. Miss 1 st on 4th row. Repeat from * to last 4 sts on 4th row. 1 sc in each of last 4 sts. Ch 3. Turn.

6th, 7th, and 8th rows: As 2nd, 3rd, and 4th rows.

9th row: Miss first 2 sts. 1 sc in each of next 3 sts. Long tr in first st of 6th row. *Miss 1 st on 8th row. 1 sc in each of next 4 sts. Miss 4 sts on 6th row. Long tr in next st. Repeat from * to end of row. Ch 3. Turn.

Repeat 2nd to 9th rows inclusive.

75. CABLE STITCH

(Multiple of 6 sts plus 2) plus 1 ch.

Foundation row: 1 sc in 2nd ch from hook. 1 sc in each ch to end of ch. Ch 3. Turn.

2nd row: Miss first st. 1 dc in next st. *Miss 2 sts. 1 tr in each of next 2 sts. Working in front of these 2 sts, 1 tr in each of 2 missed sts. 1 dc in each of next 2 sts. Repeat from * to end of row. Ch 3. Turn.

3rd row: Miss first st. 1 dc in next st. *Miss 2 sts. 1 tr in each of next 2 sts. Working behind these 2 sts, 1 tr in each of 2 missed sts. 1 dc in each of next 2 sts. Repeat from * to end of row. Ch 3. Turn.

Repeat 2nd and 3rd rows.

76. ARROW PATTERN

(Multiple of 4 sts) plus 1 ch.

Foundation row: 1 sc in 2nd ch from hook. 1 sc in each ch to end of ch. Ch 1. Turn.

2nd row: Miss first st. 1 sc in each st to end of row. Ch 3. Turn.

3rd row: Miss first st. 1 dc in next sc. *Miss 3 sc. 1 hdc in next sc. 1 dc in each of 3 missed sc. Working **behind** hdc, repeat from * ending with 1 dc in each of last 2 sc. Ch 3. Turn.

4th row: Miss first dc. 1 dc in next dc. *Miss 3 dc. 1 hdc in hdc. 1 dc in each of 3 missed dc. Working **in front of** hdc, repeat from * ending with 1 dc in each of last 2 sts. Ch 1. Turn.

5th row: Miss first dc. 1 sc in each remaining dc. Ch 1. Turn.

Repeat 2nd to 5th rows inclusive.

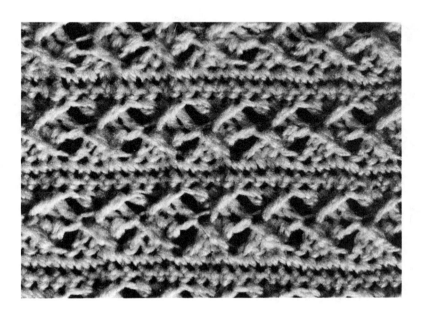

MOTIFS

Note: Motifs are pieces of crocheted fabric worked in squares, circles or hexagons, etc., and joined together when completed. Some of the following patterns are worked in two or more contrasting colours as is often seen in afghans. These motifs can be made in one colour by simply ignoring all reference to light (L), medium (M) and dark (D).

77. LACEY SQUARE

Ch 6.   Join with ss to form circle.

First round: Ch 2.   15 dc in circle.   Join with ss in top of ch 2.

2nd round: Ch 4.   *1 dc in **back loop only** of next dc. Ch 2.   Repeat from * to end of round.   Ss in 2nd st of ch 4.

3rd round: Ch 5.   1 tr in same st.   *Ch 2.   1 dc in next dc.   Ch 2.   1 hdc in next dc.   Ch 2.   1 dc in next dc.   Ch 2.   (1 tr.   Ch 2.   1 tr) in next dc.   Repeat from * twice.   Ch 2.   1 dc in next dc.   Ch 2. 1 hdc in next dc.   Ch 2.   1 dc in next dc.   Ch 2.   Ss in 3rd st of ch 5.

4th round: 3 sc in first space. 1 sc in each st, 2 sc in each space, and 3 sc in each corner space to end of round. Ss in first st. Fasten off.

78. CHECKER SQUARE

With (L) ch 6. Join with ss to form circle.

First round: Ch 2. 2 dc in circle. (Ch 3. 3 dc in circle)3 times. Ch 3. Ss in top of ch 2. Fasten off. Break (L).

2nd round: Join (D) in first space. (Ch 2. 2 dc. Ch 3. 3 dc) in first space. Ch 1. *(3 dc. Ch 3. 3 dc) in next space. Ch 1. Repeat from * twice. Ss in top of ch 2. Fasten off. Break (D).

3rd round: Join (L) in first space. (Ch 2. 2 dc. Ch 3. 3 dc) in first space. Ch 1. *3 dc in ch 1 space.

Ch 1. (3 dc. Ch 3. 3 dc) in next ch 3 space. Ch 1. Repeat from * twice. 3 dc in ch 1 space. Ch 1. Ss in top of ch 2. Fasten off. Break (L).

4th round: Join (D) in first space. (Ch 2. 2 dc. Ch 3. 3 dc) in first space. *Ch 1. 3 dc in each ch 1 space. Ch 1. (3 dc. Ch 3. 3 dc) in next ch 3 space. Ch 1. Repeat from * twice. 3 dc in next ch 1 space. Ch 1. 3 dc in last ch 1 space. Ch 1. Ss in top of ch 2. Fasten off. Break (D).

79. PETAL SQUARE

Ch 8.   Join with ss to form circle.

First round: Ch 8.   (4 dc.   Ch 5)3 times in circle.   3 dc in circle.   Ss in 3rd st of ch 8.

2nd round: *6 sc in ch 5 space.   1 sc in each dc. Repeat from * to end of round.   Ss in first sc.

3rd round: Ch 2.   1 dc in each of next 3 sts.   Ch 5. *1 dc in each of next 10 sts.   Ch 5.   Repeat from * twice.   1 dc in each of last 6 sts.   Ss in top of ch 2.

4th round: 1 sc in each st and 6 sc in each space to end of round.   Ss in first sc.

5th round: Ch 2.   1 dc in each of next 4 sts.   *Ch 3. 1 dc in each of next 16 sts.   Repeat from * twice.   Ch 3.   1 dc in each of next 11 sts.   Ss in ch 2.   Fasten off.

80. SHELL SQUARE

Ch 6.   Join with ss to form circle.

First round: Ch 2.   1 dc in circle.   (Ch 1.   4 dc in circle)3 times.   Ch 1.   2 dc in circle.

2nd round: Ss to first ch 1 space.   (Ch 2.   2 dc.   Ch 2.   3 dc) in first ch 1 space.   (3 dc.   Ch 2.   3 dc) in each of next 3 ch 1 spaces.   Ss in top of Ch 2.

3rd round: Ss to first ch 2 space.   (Ch 3.   3 tr.   Ch 3.   4 tr) in first ch 2 space.   (4 tr.   Ch 3.   4 tr) in each of next 3 ch 2 spaces.   Ss in top of ch 2.

4th round: 1 sc in each st and 4 sc in each ch 3 space to end of round.   Ss in first sc.   Fasten off.

81. CROSS SQUARE

Ch 6. Join with ss to form circle.

First round: Ch 3. 15 dc in circle. Ss in top of ch 3.

2nd round: Ch 3. Work 2 dc in same st. *Ch 2. Miss 1 dc. 1 dc in next dc. Ch 2. Miss 1 dc. 3 dc in next dc. Repeat from * twice. Ch 2. Miss 1 dc. 1 dc in next dc. Ch 2. Ss in top of ch 3.

3rd round: Ch 3. *5 dc in next dc. 1 dc in next dc. (Ch 2. 1 dc in next dc)twice. Repeat from * 3 times, ending last repeat with 1 dc. Ch 2. Ss in top of ch 3.

4th round: Ch 3. 1 dc in each of next 2 dc. *5 dc in next dc. 1 dc in each of next 3 dc. Ch 2. 1 dc in next dc. Ch 2. 1 dc in each of next 3 dc. Repeat from * 3 times, ending last repeat with 1 dc. Ch 2. Ss in top of ch 3.

5th round: Ch 3. 1 dc in first 4 dc. *5 dc in next dc. 1 dc in each of next 5 dc. Ch 2. 1 dc in next dc. Ch 2. 1 dc in each of next 5 dc. Repeat from * 3 times, ending with ch 2. Ss in top of ch 3. Fasten off.

82. OCTAGONAL MOTIF

Ch 6.   Join with ss to form circle.

First round: Ch 2.   23 dc in circle.   Ss in top of ch 2.

2nd round: Ch 4.   1 dc in same st.   Ch 1.   *Miss 2 sts.   (1 dc.   Ch 2.   1 dc) in next st.   Ch 1.   Repeat from * 6 times.   Ss in 2nd st of ch 4.

3rd round: Ch 2.   (1 dc.   Ch 2.   2 dc) in first ch 2 space.   *1 dc in ch 1 space.   (2 dc.   Ch 2.   2 dc) in next ch 2 space.   Repeat from * 6 times.   1 dc in last ch 1 space.   Ss in top of ch 2.

4th round: 1 sc in each st.   2 sc in each ch 2 space to end of round.   Ss in first sc.   Fasten off.

83. OCTAGONAL SHELLS

Ch 6.   Join with ss to form circle.

First round: Ch 2.   23 dc in circle.   Ss in top of ch 2.

2nd round: Ch 4.   1 dc in same st.   Ch 1.   *Miss 2 sts.   (1 dc.   Ch 2.   1 dc) in next st.   Ch 1.   Repeat from * 6 times.   Ss in top of ch 2.

3rd round: Ch 2.   (1 dc.   Ch 2.   2 dc) in first ch 2 space.   *Ch 1.   (2 dc.   Ch 2.   2 dc) in next ch 2 space.   Repeat from * 6 times.   Ch 1.   Ss in top of ch 2.

4th round: *7 dc for shell in ch 2 space.   1 sc in ch 1 space.   Repeat from * 7 times.   Ss in first st.   Fasten off.

84. HEXAGONAL MOTIF

With dark (D) ch 5.   Join with ss to form circle.

First round: Ch 3.   1 dc in circle.   *Ch 1.   2 dc in circle.   Repeat from * 4 times.   Ch 1.   Ss in top of ch 3.   Fasten off.

2nd round: Join medium (M) in first ch 1 space.   Ch 3.   (1 dc.   Ch 1.   2 dc) in same space.   Ch 1.   *(2 dc. Ch 1.   2 dc) for shell in next ch 1 space.   Ch 1.   Repeat from * 4 times.   Ss in top of ch 3.   Fasten off.

3rd round: Join light (L) in ch 1 space of first shell.   Ch 3.   (1 dc.   Ch 1.   2 dc) in same space.   *Ch 1. 2 dc in ch 1 space between shells.   Ch 1.   (2 dc.   Ch 1.   2 dc) in ch 1 space of next shell.   Repeat from * 4 times.   Ch 1.   2 dc in next ch 1 space.   Ch 1.   Ss in top of ch 3.   Fasten off.

4th round: Join (D) in ch 1 space of first shell.   Ch 1. 1 sc in each dc and each ch 1 space between shells. 2 sc in each ch 1 space of shells.   Join with ss in first ch 1.   Fasten off.

85. SPIDER'S WEB MOTIF

Ch 4. Join with ss to form circle.

First round: Ch 3. 17 dc in circle. Ss in top of ch 3.

2nd round: *Ch 5. Miss 2 sts. 1 sc in next st. Repeat from * 4 times. Ch 5. 1 sc in first st of ch 5.

3rd round: *Ch 7. 1 sc in next sc. Repeat from * 4 times. Ch 7. 1 sc in first st of ch 7.

4th round: *Ch 9. 1 sc in next sc. Repeat from * 4 times. Ch 9. 1 sc in first st of ch 9.

5th round: *Ch 11. 1 sc in next sc. Repeat from * 4 times. Ch 11. 1 sc in first st of ch 11.

6th round: *Ch 13. 1 sc in next sc. Repeat from * 4 times. Ch 13. 1 sc in first st of ch 13. Fasten off.

86. LACEY CIRCLE

Ch 5.   Join with ss to form circle.

First round: Ch 5.   (1 tr.   Ch 1)11 times in circle. Ss in 4th st of ch 5.

2nd round: Ch 7.   Miss 1 ch.   (1 tr in back loop only of next st.   Ch 3.   Miss 1 ch)11 times.   Ss in 4th st of ch 7.   (48 sts in round).

3rd round: (Ch 4.   Miss 3 ch.   1 sc in back loop only of next st)12 times, ending with ss in first st of ch 4.

4th round: (5 hdc in ch 4 space.   Ss in next sc)12 times.   Fasten off.

87. CIRCULAR MOTIF

Ch 5.   Join with ss to form circle.

First round: Ch 4.   15 dc in circle.   Ss in top of ch 4.

2nd round: Ch 5.   *1 dc in back loop only of next st. Ch 2.   Repeat from * to end of round.   Ss in 3rd st of ch 5.

3rd round: Ch 3.   *2 dc in next ch 2 space.   1 dc in next dc.   Ch 4.   1 dc in next dc.   Repeat from * 6 times.   2 dc in next ch 2 space.   1 dc in next dc.   Ch 4.   Ss in top of first ch 3.

4th round: Ch 1.   Working into back loops only, 1 hdc in each st of previous round.   Fasten off.

88. FLOWER MOTIF

Ch 5.   Join with ss to form circle.

First round: Ch 2.   11 hdc in circle.   Ss in top of ch 2.

2nd round: *Ch 7.   1 hdc in 2nd ch from hook.   1 hdc in each of next 4 ch.   Ss in bottom of ch.   Ss in back loop only of next 2 sts.   Repeat from * 5 times.

3rd round: *1 sc in each ch of petal.   5 sc in turning ch at top of petal.   1 sc in each hdc along other side of petal.   Ss in st between petals.   Repeat from * around each petal, ending with ss in st between last and first petal.   Fasten off.

TUNISIAN OR AFGHAN CROCHET

Note: This type of crochet is done with what is commonly known as an Afghan hook. It is a long hook similar to a knitting needle with a hook at one end and a knob at the other end. Each stitch is picked up and retained on the hook from right to left across the row, then worked off the hook from left to right, and these two processes form one row. Most patterns start with first two rows as given in Basic Afghan Stitch.

89. BASIC AFGHAN STITCH
**Make a chain of desired number of stitches.

First row: Insert hook into 2nd ch from hook. *Yoh and draw through a loop. Repeat from * in each ch to end of ch retaining all loops on hook. **Do not turn.**

2nd row: Yoh and draw loop through first st on hook. *Yoh and draw through next 2 loops on hook. Repeat from * to end of row. (1 loop left on hook.) Ch 1.**

3rd row: *Insert hook under vertical st from right to left. Yoh and draw through a loop. Repeat from * to end of row retaining all loops on hook.

4th row: As 2nd row.

Repeat 3rd and 4th rows.

90. PLAIN AFGHAN STITCH

Work from ** to ** as given in Basic Afghan Stitch.

3rd row: *Insert hook under st between vertical sts of previous row. Yoh and draw through a loop. Repeat from * to end of row.

4th row: As 2nd row of Basic Afghan Stitch.

Repeat 3rd and 4th rows.

91. FANCY AFGHAN STITCH

Work from ** to ** as given in Basic Afghan Stitch.

3rd row: *Insert hook **in** st between vertical sts of previous row. Yoh and draw through a loop. Repeat from * to end of row.

4th row: As 2nd row of Basic Afghan Stitch.

Repeat 3rd and 4th rows.

92. KNITTED STITCH

Work from ** to ** as given in Basic Afghan Stitch.

3rd row: *Insert hook between the 2 double vertical sts from front to back. Yoh and draw through a loop. Repeat from * to end of row.

4th row: As 2nd row of Basic Afghan Stitch.

Repeat 3rd and 4th rows.

93. PURL STITCH

Make a chain of desired number of sts.

First row: *With yarn at front of work, insert hook from back through ch with yarn under hook and draw through a loop. Repeat from * to end of ch retaining all sts on hook.

2nd row: As 2nd row of Basic Afghan Stitch.

3rd row: *With yarn at front of work, insert hook from right to left through vertical st of previous row. Yoh and draw through a loop. Repeat from * to end of row.

4th row: As 2nd row.

Repeat 3rd and 4th rows.

94. RIBBED STITCH

(Multiple of 4 sts).

Work as given from ** to ** in Basic Afghan Stitch.

3rd row: *2 sts as given in 3rd row of Basic Afghan Stitch. 2 sts as 3rd row of Purl Stitch. Repeat from * to end of row.

4th row: As 2nd row of Basic Afghan Stitch.

Repeat 3rd and 4th rows.

95. CLUSTER STITCH

(Multiple of 4 sts plus 1).

Make a chain of desired length and work first row as given in Basic Afghan Stitch.

2nd row: *Ch 3. Yoh and draw through 5 loops to make cluster. Yoh and draw through 1 loop. Repeat from * to end of row. Ch 1.

3rd row: *Insert hook through top of cluster. Yoh and draw through a loop. Insert hook through each ch st and draw through a loop. Repeat from * to end of row.

4th row: As 2nd row.

Repeat 3rd and 4th rows.

96. LACEY STITCH

(Multiple of 2 sts plus 1).

First row: Insert hook in 3rd ch from hook. Yoh and draw through a loop. *Ch 1. Miss 1 ch. Insert hook in next ch. Yoh and draw through a loop. Repeat from * to end of ch.

2nd row: As 2nd row of Basic Afghan Stitch, drawing yarn through first loop. *Ch 1. Yoh and draw through 2 loops. Repeat from * to end of row. Ch 1.

3rd row: *Insert hook through vertical st of previous row. Yoh and draw through a loop. Ch 1. Repeat from * to end of row.

4th row: As 2nd row.

Repeat 3rd and 4th rows.

EDGINGS

Note: A crochet edging can do a great deal to enhance the appearance of the finished fabric whether that fabric is knitted or crocheted. In the case of garments such as dresses, pullovers, etc., some form of edging is nearly always required around the neck and armholes to give the garment a good firm fit. An edging also hides any uneven spots at the edge of the fabric caused by increasing or decreasing.

A garment made with a fancy or lacey stitch pattern is usually edged with just one or two rows of plain single crochet which will give it a firmer edge without detracting from the fabric itself. If the fabric is made in a plain stitch, a picot or shell edging can lend a note of interest to the finished article.

Note that the edgings shown here are worked on flat pieces of fabric that have not been joined, so that the rows of edging are worked with a turn at each end of rows.

For edging armholes, necklines, or lower edges of garments, when the seams have been joined, the edging can be worked in rounds on the **right** side of the work without turning.

When working edging around corners, work three stitches into each corner stitch so that the corner will lie flat.

97. PICOT EDGING

With wrong side of work facing, join yarn at side edge and work 1 row sc. Turn.

2nd row: *Ch 3. 1 sc in 3rd ch from hook to form picot. 1 sc in each of next 2 sts. Repeat from * to end of row. Fasten off.

Note: Picots can be spaced further apart if desired, but care must be taken to have the correct multiple of sts so that the last picot will be in end st to correspond to first picot.

98. SHELL EDGING

(Multiple of 5 sts).

With wrong side of work facing, join yarn at side edge and work 1 row sc. Ch 4. Turn.

2nd row: 1 dc in first st. *Miss 4 sts. (1 dc. Ch 1)3 times. 1 dc for shell in next st. Repeat from * to last 5 sts. Miss 4 sts. (1 dc. Ch 1. 1 dc) in last st. Fasten off.

99. FANCY EDGING

(Multiple of 6 sts plus 1).

With right side of work facing, join yarn at side edge of work and work along edge to be trimmed as follows: 1 sc in first st. *Miss 2 sts. (1 dc. Ch 3. Ss in 3rd ch from hook for picot)3 times, 1 dc all in next st. Miss 2 sts. 1 sc in next st. Repeat from * to end of row. Fasten off.

100. CLUSTER EDGING

With right side of work facing, join yarn at side edge of work and work along edge to be trimmed as follows: Ch 3. *In next st (yoh and draw up a loop)4 times. Yoh and draw through all 9 loops. Yoh and draw through last loop to form cluster. Miss 1 st. Repeat from * ending with cluster in last st. Fasten off.

101. RUFFLES

With wrong side of work facing, join yarn at side edge and work along edge to be trimmed as follows:

First row: Ch 4. *Miss 2 sts. 1 dc in next st. Ch 2. Repeat from * ending with 1 dc in last st. Turn.

2nd row: It is usual to work through the **top** of each st. To make ruffles, the **length** of the stitch is used and is called the 'post'. Work 5 dc down first post. *Ch 1. Work 5 dc down next post. Repeat from * to end of row. Fasten off.

Note: For a wider ruffle, work trebles instead of doubles in row, and work 7 dc in each post.

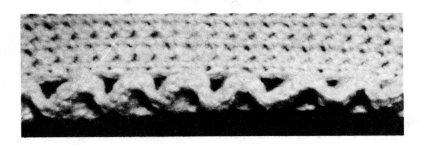

102. CORDED OR ITALIAN EDGE

With right side of work facing, work 1 row sc. **Do not turn.**

2nd row: Ch 1. Working from left to right instead of from right to left as usual, work 1 sc in each st of previous row. Fasten off.

103. FRINGES

Wind yarn over a piece of cardboard 5 or 6 inches wide (or desired width) and cut through one edge. Take 3 strands together, double them, and with a crochet hook draw them through first st of edge. Pass the ends through the loop and knot firmly.

Repeat at even distances along edge. Trim evenly.

104. TASSELS

Wind yarn over a piece of cardboard 5 or 6 inches wide (or desired width) about 10 times. Remove from cardboard and tie tightly around all strands about one-half inch from end. Using a bodkin, thread end of yarn through top of tassel and secure ends of loops tightly and sew to edge of work. Cut through other end of tassel and trim evenly.

105. LOOPED FRINGE

With wrong side of work facing, join yarn at side edge and work 1 row sc along edge to be trimmed.   Ch 1. Turn.

2nd row: 1 sc in first st.   *Ch 18.   1 sc in next st. Repeat from * to end of row. Fasten off. **Note:** Length of edging may be changed by adjusting number of ch sts.

106. CHAIN FRINGE

With wrong side of work facing, join yarn at side edge and work 1 row sc along edge to be trimmed. Ch 1. Turn.

2nd row: Ss in first st. *Ch 12 sts. Turn. Work back along ch working 1 ss in each ch st. Ss in next st. Repeat from * to end of row. Fasten off. **Note:** Length of edging may be changed by adjusting number of ch sts.